SWIFTER THAN EAGLES

THE BIBLICAL MIDDLE EAST AT WAR

Written by Richard Bodley Scott, assisted
by Nik Gaukroger, James Hamilton,
Paul Robinson, Thom Richardson
and Duncan Head

OSPREY
PUBLISHING   SLITHERINE

First published in Great Britain in 2009 by Osprey Publishing Ltd.

Osprey Publishing, Midland House, West Way, Botley, Oxford OX2 0PH, UK
443 Park Avenue South, New York, NY 10016, USA
E-mail: info@ospreypublishing.com

Slitherine Software UK Ltd., The White Cottage, 8 West Hill Avenue, Epsom, KT 19 8LE, UK
E-mail: info@slitherine.co.uk

A CIP catalogue record for this book is available from the British Library

ISBN: 978 1 84603 480 0

Rules system written by Richard Bodley Scott, Simon Hall, and Terry Shaw
Page layout and cover concept by Myriam Bell
Index by Michael Parkin
Project Management by JD McNeil and Osprey Team Technical management by Iain McNeill
Typeset in Joanna Pro and Sleepy Hollow
Cover artwork by Peter Dennis
Photography by Duncan MacFarlane – Wargames Illustrated, Don McHugh, Simon Davey, Anthony Winter
Page design features supplied by istockphoto.com
All artwork and cartography © Osprey Publishing Ltd
Originated by PDQ Media, UK
Printed in China through Worldprint Ltd

09 10 11 12 13   10 9 8 7 6 5 4 3 2 1

FOR A CATALOGUE OF ALL BOOKS PUBLISHED BY OSPREY MILITARY
AND AVIATION PLEASE CONTACT:

NORTH AMERICA
Osprey Direct, c/o Random House Distribution Center, 400 Hahn Road,
Westminster, MD 21157
E-mail: uscustomerservice@ospreypublishing.com

ALL OTHER REGIONS
Osprey Direct, The Book Service Ltd, Distribution Centre, Colchester Road,
Frating Green, Colchester, Essex, CO7 7DW
E-mail: customerservice@ospreypublishing.com

FOR DETAILS OF ALL GAMES PUBLISHED BY SLITHERINE SOFTWARE UK LTD
E-mail: info@slitherine.co.uk

Osprey Publishing is supporting the Woodland Trust, the UK's leading woodland
conservation charity, by funding the dedication of trees.

www.ospreypublishing.com
www.slitherine.com

CONTENTS

INTRODUCTION

This book covers the better known armies of the Near East in the Bronze and Iron Ages up until the creation of the Achaemenid Persian Empire in the mid-6th century BC.

Metallurgy developed first in the mountains of the Anatolian highlands (in modern Turkey), where there were rich deposits of metal ores. The Early Bronze Age (3500–2000 BC) saw the rise of urbanisation with the creation of city states throughout the "Fertile Crescent" from Egypt to Mesopotamia (modern Iraq) and the development of larger kingdoms such as those of Egypt and Akkad. The Middle Bronze Age (2000–1600) saw major movements of peoples, such as the Amorites, Hittites, Hurrians and Hyksos, changing the political map. The development of true chariots towards the end of this period revolutionised warfare. The Late Bronze Age (1600–1200) saw the great kingdoms – Egypt, the Hittites, Mitanni, Assyria and Babylon – competing for power on a grand scale.

In the late 13th and early 12th centuries, however, there appears to have been a major crisis throughout the Near East, resulting in the complete collapse of the Aegean (Mycenaean) and Anatolian (Hittite) palace cultures and the retreat of the Egyptian Kingdom to its core territory. The causes of this collapse are disputed, but there is no doubt that the period saw major migrations of militant peoples throughout the Mediterranean region, particularly the enigmatic "Sea Peoples".

The Ancient Near East, c.9th century BC. Taken from Essential Histories 67: Ancient Israel at War 853–586 BC.

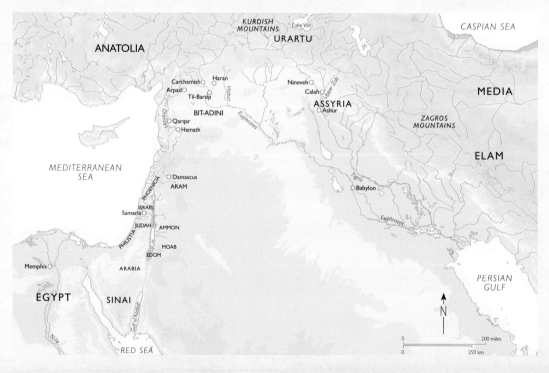

Sea People Army on the march

After these convulsions had run their course, at the start of the Iron Age, most of the Near East was once more divided up into a patchwork of small kingdoms, even Egypt being relatively weak and divided. The development (or increased use) of cavalry in the early 9th century, accompanied by an increase in the weight, crew size and number of horses of chariots, saw a further change in the character of warfare.

The gradual rise in power of the Kingdom of Assyria, though opposed by Babylon and Elam in the south-east, the newly formed Kingdom of Urartu in the north and the various Neo-Hittite and Aramaean kingdoms of Syria and Canaan in the west, was ultimately inexorable. The Assyrian Empire reached the peak of its power in the mid-7th century, only to be wiped off the map by the Medes and Babylonians before the end of the century. From then until the mid-6th century, the Near East was divided between the mighty Median and Babylonian Empires and the Kingdoms of Lydia (in western Anatolia) and Egypt. The Achaemenid Cyrus (Kūruš) II the

Great put an end to all this by taking over the Median Empire (550) and conquering Lydia (546) and Babylon (539). His son Cambyses (Kambūjia) II conquered Egypt (525). The Persian Empire then ruled the whole of the Near East from Egypt and the Aegean to India. Only the city states of Greece remained independent – but that is another story.

TROOP NOTES

There is evidence that chariot runners, infantry trained to cooperate closely with chariots, were used by Egyptians, Hittites, Mitanni, Israelites and Mycenaeans. Given the patchy nature of the evidence available for the period, it is therefore likely that they were a standard feature of the Late Bronze Age chariot system. Their tactical function is unknown – we can only speculate. We do not represent them separately but include them as part of the formation making up each light chariot base. If desired they can be depicted as infantry figures on the same bases as the chariots.

NUBIAN

Nubia (in northern modern Sudan) was the area along the Nile south of Egypt, from the First Cataract southwards. The main trade routes from tropical Africa passed through it to Egypt, carrying gold, ivory, ebony and incense. Lower (northern) Nubians were similar in physical appearance to Egyptians, though somewhat darker skinned. Upper (southern) Nubians had a more Black African appearance.

During the Egyptian Middle Kingdom, the Egyptians annexed Lower Nubia, erecting a chain of fortresses along the Nile up to the Second Cataract. By the mid-19th century BC the Pharaoh Senusret III had established the frontier at Semna, south of the Second Cataract.

Nubian General

At the end of the Middle Kingdom, control of the region was lost. At the beginning of the New Kingdom in the mid-16th century BC, however, Lower Nubia was gradually reconquered. By the end of the reign of Thutmose I, the border had been moved south to the Fourth Cataract.

This list covers Nubian armies from 3000 BC to the early 15th century BC.

TROOP NOTES

Most Nubian tribesmen were archers, but some are depicted with shield and club instead, or javelins.

Clothing was scanty and made of animal skins, often exotic. Ostrich feathers were often worn in the hair.

Nubian Javelinman

NUBIAN STARTER ARMY		
Commander-in-Chief	1	Field Commander
Sub-commanders	2	2 x Troop Commander
Close fighters	2 BGs	Each comprising 8 bases of close fighters: Superior, Protected, Undrilled Medium Foot – Swordsmen
Archers	8 BGs	Each comprising 8 bases of archers: Average, Unprotected, Undrilled Light Foot – Bow
Javelinmen	1 BG	8 bases of javelinmen: Average, Unprotected, Undrilled Light Foot – Javelins, Light Spear
Camp	1	Unfortified camp
Total	11 BGs	Camp, 88 foot bases, 3 commanders

BUILDING A CUSTOMISED LIST USING OUR ARMY POINTS

Choose an army based on the maxima and minima in the list below. The following special instructions apply to this army:

• Commanders should be depicted as archers.

NUBIAN

Territory Types: Agricultural, Hilly

Troop name		Troop Type				Capabilities		Points per base	Bases per BG	Total bases
		Type	Armour	Quality	Training	Shooting	Close Combat			
C-in-C		Inspired Commander/Field Commander/Troop Commander						80/50/35		1
Sub-commanders		Field Commander						50	0-2	
		Troop Commander						35	0-3	
Core Troops										
Archers		Light Foot	Unprotected	Average	Undrilled	Bow	-	5	6-8	40-186
		Medium Foot	Unprotected	Average	Undrilled	Bow	-	5	6-8	
Optional Troops										
Close Fighters with axe or club		Medium Foot	Protected	Superior	Undrilled	-	Swordsmen	8	6-8	0-16
				Average				6		
Javelinmen		Light Foot	Unprotected	Average	Drilled	Javelins	Light Spear	4	6-8	0-24

EARLY LIBYAN

Ancient Libya was the region west of Egypt. The most important Libyan tribes, from an Egyptian viewpoint, were the Tjehenu, the Tjemehu, the Libu and the Meshwesh. These peoples seem to have been of varied ethnic origin – for example the Tjehenu were similar to Egyptians but the Tjemehu had fair hair and pale skins.

Climatic change resulting in the expansion of the Sahara Desert caused population pressure on the Libyan tribes, resulting in increasing raids into Egypt. At the end of the 13th century BC the Libyan tribes formed a large coalition and invaded Egypt

Libyan Javelinman

in alliance with the Sea Peoples (see page 44). They were defeated by the Pharaoh Merenptah. Somewhat over a quarter of a century later, Ramesses III was forced to repel two further major Libyan invasions in the 6th and 11th years of his reign. He also, in his 8th year, defeated a major coalition of Sea Peoples.

The strength of the Egyptian state was much weakened by these wars. Large numbers of Libyans were recruited into the army and located in military settlements. They developed into a military caste, named after the tribe of the Meshwesh. In the mid-10th century BC, Libyan dynasties took control in Lower Egypt and ruled for over 200 years. Their armies are covered by the Libyan Egyptian list (see page 54).

This list covers Libyan tribal armies from 3000 to 550 BC.

Libyan–Egyptian border skirmish, by Angus McBride. Taken from Elite 40: New Kingdom Egypt.

TROOP NOTES

The earliest Libyan armies fought entirely on foot, using bows, javelins and throw-sticks. They did not use shields, but some wore a heavy animal-skin or cloth cloak that must have provided very limited protection. Apart from that they were mostly naked except for a phallus sheath. Their skin was sometimes painted or tattooed. They were bearded and often wore ostrich plumes in their hair, which was plaited into dreadlocks, sometimes dressed in mud.

In the later 13th century BC they started to use chariots and "copper" swords of Sea Peoples design. The only weapons clearly shown in any of the Libyan chariots on Ramesses III's Medinet Habu relief are bows. Later, in the Classical period, Libyans are reported as fielding very large numbers of chariots. Libyan graffiti of the later period show chariot crew armed with spears.

Libyan infantry of the period of Ramesses III are depicted as mostly swordsmen and archers. Recorded loot from one Egyptian victory included 603 bows, 2310 quivers, and only 92 spears. In the Classical Period Libyan infantry were mostly javelinmen.

Libyan Archer

LIBYAN STARTER ARMY		
Commander-in-Chief	1	Field Commander
Sub-commanders	2	2 x Troop Commander
Chariots	2 BGs	Each comprising 4 bases of chariots: Superior, Undrilled Light Chariots – Bow
Swordsmen	4 BGs	Each comprising 8 bases of swordsmen: Average, Unprotected, Undrilled Medium Foot – Impact Foot, Swordsmen
Archers	5 BGs	Each comprising 6 bases of archers: Average, Unprotected, Undrilled Light Foot – Bow
Camp	1	Unfortified camp
Total	11 BGs	Camp, 8 mounted bases, 62 foot bases, 3 commanders

BUILDING A CUSTOMISED LIST USING OUR ARMY POINTS

Choose an army based on the maxima and minima in the list below. The following special instructions apply to this army:

- Commanders should be depicted in chariots or as swordsmen or javelinmen.

Libyan Swordsman

EARLY LIBYAN

Territory Types: Desert

C-in-C	Inspired	Commander/Field Commander/Troop Commander				80/50/35		1
Sub-commanders		Field Commander				50		0-2
		Troop Commander				35		0-3

Troop name		Troop Type				Capabilities		Points per base	Bases per BG	Total bases
		Type	Armour	Quality	Training	Shooting	Close Combat			
Core Troops										
Chariots	Only from 1250 to 651	Light Chariots	-	Superior	Undrilled	-	Bow	17	4-6	4-12
	Only from 650	Light Chariots	-	Superior	Undrilled	-	Light Spear	15	4-6	8-32
Swordsmen	Only from 1208 to 651	Medium Foot	Unprotected	Average	Undrilled	-	Impact Foot, Swordsmen	6	8-12	16-60
Javelinmen		Light Foot	Unprotected	Average	Undrilled	Javelins	Light Spear	4	6-8	Before 650 0-128, From 650 32-128
		Medium Foot	Unprotected	Average	Undrilled	-	Light Spear	4	6-8	
Archers		Light Foot	Unprotected	Average	Undrilled	Bow	-	5	6-8	Before 650 16-128, From 650 0-32
		Medium Foot	Unprotected	Average	Undrilled	Bow	-	5	6-8	
Allies										

Sea Peoples allies (Only from 1208 to 1176)

EARLY LIBYAN ALLIES

Allied commander		Field Commander/Troop Commander						40/25		1
Troop name		Troop Type				Capabilities		Points per base	Bases per BG	Total bases
		Armour	Quality	Training	Shooting	Close Combat	Close Combat			
Chariots	Only from 1250 to 651	Light Chariots	-	Superior	Undrilled	-	Bow	17	4	0-4
	Only from 650	Light Chariots	-	Superior	Undrilled	-	Light Spear	15	4-6	4-12
Swordsmen	Only from 1208 to 651	Medium Foot	Unprotected	Average	Undrilled	-	Impact Foot, Swordsmen	6	8-12	8-20
Javelinmen		Light Foot	Unprotected	Average	Undrilled	Javelins	Light Spear	4	6-8	Before 650 0-40, From 650 8-40
		Medium Foot	Unprotected	Average	Undrilled	-	Light Spear	4	6-8	
Archers		Light Foot	Unprotected	Average	Undrilled	Bow	-	5	6-8	Before 650 6-40, From 650 0-8
		Medium Foot	Unprotected	Average	Undrilled	Bow	-	5	6-8	

LATER SUMERIAN OR AKKADIAN

Sumer and Akkad were situated in what is now southern Iraq. Sumer was in the south and Akkad to the north. Both areas shared a common culture, but the Sumerians spoke an agglutinative language, whereas the Akkadian language was Semitic. The region is naturally arid, but massive irrigation systems were developed by the early cities, allowing intensive agriculture of the fertile soil of the alluvial plains of the lower Tigris and Euphrates.

Sumer was divided into a number of rival city-states, each of which had its own patron god. Wars between the city states were common from an early date. Often the ruler of one city gained supremacy over a number of other cities and could mobilise their combined forces under his command.

Sargon the Great of Akkad (reigned c.2334–2279 BC) created the world's first great empire, not only conquering the whole of Mesopotamia, but campaigning as far as Syria and Canaan in the west, Elam in the east, and Magan (Oman) in the south. Armies of the Akkadian Empire probably numbered in the region of 20,000 men. After existing for little over 100 years, however, the Akkadian Empire collapsed c.2193 as a result of invasion by Gutian tribesmen from the Zagros Mountains to the east.

Following a period of anarchy, the Third Dynasty of Ur rose to prominence c.2112. It fell to an Elamite invasion c.2004. Following this, the Kingdom of Isin carried on Sumero-Akkadian culture. Meanwhile many of the nomadic Amorite

Sumerian chariot of King Eannatum of Lagash, c.2500 BC, by Angus McBride.
Taken from Men-at-Arms 109: Ancient Armies of the Middle East.

tribes who had been settling in Mesopotamia and Syria since c.2500 gave up the nomadic life, created their own kingdoms and became culturally assimilated. One such kingdom, Larsa, soon rivalled the power of Isin.

This list covers Sumerian and Akkadian armies from the start of the Sumerian Early Dynastic II period c.2800, through the Akkadian Empire period (c.2334–2193) until the destruction of the Third Dynasty of Ur by the Elamites c.2004, and then the various successor states of the Isin-Larsa period until c.1762 BC.

TROOP NOTES

In the early part of the period, the only protection of the spearmen was a thick felt or leather cloak. At some point in the early 25th century BC, they started to carry large body shields for the front ranks. Akkadian spearmen often discarded their shields to fight in difficult terrain. From the mid-21st century a smaller, less unwieldy shield of Amorite origin came into use.

Battle cars and platform cars are rated as undrilled to reflect their unwieldiness.

THIRD DYNASTY OF UR STARTER ARMY

Commander-in-Chief	1	Field Commander
Sub-commanders	2	2 x Troop Commander
Proto-chariots	1 BG	4 bases of proto-chariots: Average, Undrilled Light Chariots – Light Spear
Retained spearmen	2 BGs	Each comprising 8 bases of retained spearmen: Superior, Protected, Drilled Medium Foot – Offensive Spearmen
Militia spearmen	3 BGs	Each comprising 8 bases of militia spearmen: Average, Protected, Drilled Heavy Foot – Defensive Spearmen
Archers	2 BGs	Each comprising 6 bases of archers: Average, Unprotected, Undrilled Light Foot – Bow
Slingers	1 BG	6 bases of slingers: Average, Unprotected, Undrilled Light Foot – Sling
Javelinmen	1 BG	6 bases of javelinmen: Average, Unprotected, Undrilled Light Foot – Javelins, Light Spear
Camp	1	Unfortified camp
Total	10 BGs	Camp, 4 mounted bases, 64 foot bases, 3 commanders

BUILDING A CUSTOMISED LIST USING OUR ARMY POINTS

Choose an army based on the maxima and minima in the list below. The following special instructions apply to this army:

- Commanders should be depicted on 2-wheeled straddle or platform car, in 4-wheeled battle car or as royal guard axemen.

- A Sumerian or Akkadian allied commander's contingent must conform to the Later Sumerian or Akkadian list below, but the troops in the contingent are deducted from the minima and maxima in the main list.

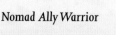

Nomad Ally Warrior

LATER SUMERIAN OR AKKADIAN

Territory Types: Developed, Agricultural. Only Akkadians: Hilly

C-in-C	Inspired Commander/Field Commander/Troop Commander						80/50/35	1	
Sub-commanders	Field Commander						50	0-2	
	Troop Commander						35	0-3	
Sumerian or Akkadian allied commanders	Field Commander/Troop Commander						40/25	0-3	

Troop name		Troop Type				Capabilities		Points per base	Bases per BG	Total bases
		Type	Armour	Quality	Training	Shooting	Close Combat			
Core Troops										
Royal guardsmen with heavy axe		Heavy Foot	Unprotected	Superior	Drilled	-	Heavy Weapon	8	6-8	0-8
Retained archers		Medium Foot	Unprotected	Superior	Drilled	Bow	-	7	6-8	0-8
				Average				6		
Retained spearmen	Only before 2500	Heavy Foot	Unprotected	Superior	Drilled		Defensive Spearmen	7	6-8	6-16
				Average				6		
	Only from 2500	Heavy Foot	Protected	Superior	Drilled		Defensive Spearmen	9	6-8	
				Average				7		
	Only from 2500 to 2051	Medium Foot	Unprotected	Superior	Drilled		Offensive Spearmen	8	6-8	
				Average				7		
	Only from 2050	Medium Foot	Protected	Superior	Drilled		Offensive Spearmen	10	6-8	
				Average				8		
Militia spearmen	Only before 2500	Heavy Foot	Unprotected	Average	Drilled		Defensive Spearmen	6	6-10	18-102
				Poor				4		
	Only from 2500	Heavy Foot	Protected	Average	Drilled		Defensive Spearmen	7	6-10	
				Poor				5		
Archers		Light Foot	Unprotected	Average	Undrilled	Bow	-	5	6-8	0-18
		Light Foot	Unprotected	Poor	Undrilled	Bow	-	3	6-8	0-8
Slingers		Light Foot	Unprotected	Average	Undrilled	Sling	-	4	6-8	0-18
		Light Foot	Unprotected	Poor	Undrilled	Sling	-	2	6-8	0-8
Javelinmen		Light Foot	Unprotected	Average	Undrilled	Javelins	Light Spear	4	6-8	0-12
		Medium Foot	Unprotected	Average	Undrilled	-	Light Spear	4		
		Light Foot	Unprotected	Poor	Undrilled	Javelins	Light Spear	2	6-8	0-8
		Medium Foot	Unprotected	Poor	Undrilled	-	Light Spear	2	6-8	
Optional Troops										
4-wheeled battle cars	Only before 2334	Heavy Chariots	-	Average	Undrilled	-	Light Spear	14	4-6	0-8
	Only from 2334 to 2193	Heavy Chariots	-	Average	Undrilled	-	Light Spear	14	4	0-4
4-equid platform cars or 2-equid proto-chariots	Only from 2334	Light Chariots	-	Average	Undrilled	-	Light Spear	11	4	0-4
Hastily raised levies		Mob	Unprotected	Poor	Undrilled	-	-	2	8-12	0-12
Amorites	Only from 2500	Medium Foot	Protected	Average	Undrilled	-	Light Spear	5	6-8	0-16
		Medium Foot	Protected	Average	Undrilled	-	Light Spear, Swordsmen	6		
Fortified camp								24		0-1
Field fortifications		Field Fortifications						3		0-12
Allies										

Amorite allies (Only from 2500) – up to 2 contingents – Early Nomad

LATER SUMERIAN OR AKKADIAN ALLIES

Allied commander		Field Commander/Troop Commander						40/25		1		
Troop name		**Troop Type**				**Capabilities**		**Points per base**	**Bases per BG**	**Total bases**		
		Type	Armour	Quality	Training	Shooting	Close Combat					
Retained spearmen	Only before 2500	Heavy Foot	Unprotected	Superior	Drilled	-	Defensive Spearmen	7	4-6	0-6		
				Average				6				
	Only from 2500	Heavy Foot	Protected	Superior	Drilled	-	Defensive Spearmen	9	4-6			
				Average				7				
	Only from 2500 to 2051	Medium Foot	Unprotected	Superior	Drilled	-	Offensive Spearmen	8	4-6			
				Average				7				
	Only from 2050	Medium Foot	Protected	Superior	Drilled	-	Offensive Spearmen	10	4-6			
				Average				8				
Militia spearmen	Only before 2500	Heavy Foot	Unprotected	Average	Drilled	-	Defensive Spearmen	6	6-10	6-24		
				Poor				4				
	Only from 2500	Heavy Foot	Protected	Average	Drilled	-	Defensive Spearmen	7	6-10			
				Poor				5				
Archers		Light Foot	Unprotected	Average	Undrilled	Bow	-	5	6-8	0-8		0-12
				Poor				3				
Slingers		Light Foot	Unprotected	Average	Undrilled	Sling	-	4	6-8	0-8		
				Poor				2				
Javelinmen		Light Foot	Unprotected	Average	Undrilled	Javelins	Light Spear	4	4-6	0-6		
				Poor				2				
		Medium Foot	Unprotected	Average	Undrilled	-	Light Spear	4				
				Poor				2				

EARLY NOMAD ALLIES

Allied commander	Field Commander/Troop Commander						40/25		1	
Troop name	**Troop Type**				**Capabilities**		**Points per base**	**Bases per BG**	**Total bases**	
	Type	Armour	Quality	Training	Shooting	Close Combat				
Warriors	Medium Foot	Unprotected	Average	Undrilled	-	Light Spear	4	6-8	8-32	
	Medium Foot	Protected	Average	Undrilled	-	Light Spear	5			
	Medium Foot	Protected	Average	Undrilled	-	Light Spear, Swordsmen	6			
Skirmishers	Light Foot	Unprotected	Average	Undrilled	Javelins	Light Spear	4	4-6	0-8	
	Light Foot	Unprotected	Average	Undrilled	Bow	-	5			
	Light Foot	Unprotected	Average	Undrilled	Sling	-	4			

OLD OR MIDDLE KINGDOM EGYPTIAN

The Egyptian Old Kingdom is usually taken as the period of the 3rd, 4th, 5th and 6th dynasties from c.2686 to 2181 BC. Some historians also include the 7th and 8th dynasties. During this period the capital was at Memphis. It was during the Old Kingdom that most of the pyramids were built. Towards the end of the period the power of the nomarchs (regional governors) increased at the expense of the central authority. During the possibly 94 year reign of Pepi II (the longest recorded reign in world history) the country was severely afflicted with droughts, and following his death the kingdom fell apart.

This ushered in the First Intermediate Period, a period of relative anarchy and cultural decline. Circa 2050, Mentuhotep II, of the 11th dynasty, reunited Egypt, ushering in the Middle Kingdom. During the Middle Kingdom, Egyptian hegemony was expanded southwards into Lower (northern) Nubia, reaching beyond the Second

Middle Kingdom Archer

Cataract of the Nile, and eastwards into Palestine and Lebanon.

After the end of the 12th dynasty, c.1802, the country once again became divided. The 13th dynasty gradually lost control over Egypt, ushering in the Second Intermediate Period. A rival 14th dynasty appeared in the Nile Delta. Circa 1650 the (possibly Amorite) Hyksos took control of Lower (northern) Egypt and set themselves up as the 15th (and possibly 16th) dynasty which lasted until c.1535. In Upper (southern) Egypt the native 17th dynasty ruled from Thebes from c.1650 to 1550.

Near the end of the 17th dynasty, the Theban pharaohs began a war of reconquest against the Hyksos. Ahmose I, the first pharaoh of the 18th dynasty, who reigned from c.1550 to 1525, completed this and reunited the kingdom. This ushered in the period of the greatest Egyptian glory, the New Kingdom.

This list covers the armies of the 3rd to 17th dynasties of Egypt from c.2686 to 1550 BC, excluding the 15th and 16th dynasties which are covered by the Hyksos list.

MIDDLE KINGDOM EGYPTIAN STARTER ARMY		
Commander-in-Chief	1	Field Commander
Sub-commanders	2	2 x Troop Commander
Elite close fighters	2 BGs	Each comprising 8 bases of elite close fighters: Superior, Protected, Drilled Heavy Foot – Heavy Weapon
Close fighters	2 BGs	Each comprising 8 bases of close fighters: Average, Protected, Drilled Medium Foot – Swordsmen
Conscript spearmen	1 BG	8 bases of conscript spearmen: Poor, Protected, Undrilled Medium Foot – Light Spear
Archers	2 BGs	Each comprising 8 bases of archers: Average, Unprotected, Drilled, Medium Foot – Bow
Nubian archers	2 BGs	Each comprising 6 bases of Nubian archers: Average, Unprotected, Undrilled Light Foot – Bow
Bedouin slingers	1 BG	6 bases of Bedouin slingers: Average, Unprotected, Undrilled Light Foot – Sling
Camp	1	Unfortified camp
Total	10 BGs	Camp, 74 foot bases, 3 commanders

Middle Kingdom Egypt at war, by Peter Bull. Taken from Warrior 121: Soldier of the Pharaoh: Middle Kingdom Egypt 2055–1650 BC.

OLD OR MIDDLE KINGDOM EGYPTIAN

BUILDING A CUSTOMISED LIST USING OUR ARMY POINTS

Choose an army based on the maxima and minima in the list below. The following special instructions apply to this army:

- Commanders should be depicted as close

fighters, or, from 1640, in light chariots.

- Close fighters can interpenetrate archers and vice versa.

Middle Kingdom Close Fighter

OLD OR MIDDLE KINGDOM EGYPTIAN

Territory Types: Developed, Agricultural

C-in-C	Inspired Commander/Field Commander/Troop Commander						80/50/35		1	
Sub-commanders	Field Commander						50		0-2	
	Troop Commander						35		0-3	
Troop name	Troop Type				Capabilities		Points per base	Bases per BG	Total bases	
	Type	Armour	Quality	Training	Shooting	Close Combat				
Core Troops										
Elite close fighters with 2-handed eye-axe	Heavy Foot	Protected	Superior	Drilled	-	Heavy Weapon	10	6-8	6-16	
Close fighters with one-handed eye-axe or club	Medium Foot	Protected	Average	Drilled	-	Swordsmen	7	6-8	8-40	
Archers	Medium Foot	Unprotected	Average	Drilled	Bow	-	6	6-8	12-64	
Conscript spearmen	Medium Foot	Protected	Poor	Undrilled	-	Light Spear	3	8-12	8-48	
Optional Troops										
Javelinmen	Medium Foot	Protected	Average	Drilled	-	Light spear	6	6-8	0-8	
	Light Foot	Unprotected	Average	Drilled	Javelins	Light Spear	4	6-8		
Nubian archers	Light Foot	Unprotected	Superior	Undrilled	Bow	-	6	6-8	0-16	
			Average				5			
	Medium Foot	Unprotected	Superior	Undrilled	Bow	-	6	6-8		
			Average				5			
Libyan javelinmen	Light Foot	Unprotected	Average	Undrilled	Javelins	Light Spear	4	6-8	0-8	
Bedouin slingers	Light Foot	Unprotected	Average	Undrilled	Sling	-	4	4-6	0-6	

OLD OR MIDDLE KINGDOM EGYPTIAN ALLIES

Allied commander	Field Commander/Troop Commander						40/25		1	
Troop name	Troop Type				Capabilities		Points per base	Bases per BG	Total bases	
	Type	Armour	Quality	Training	Shooting	Close Combat				
Elite close fighters with 2-handed eye-axe	Heavy Foot	Protected	Superior	Drilled	-	Heavy Weapon	10	4-6	0-6	
Close fighters with one-handed eye-axe or club	Medium Foot	Protected	Average	Drilled	-	Swordsmen	7	6-8	6-12	
Archers	Medium Foot	Unprotected	Average	Drilled	Bow	-	6	6-8	6-18	
Conscript spearmen	Medium Foot	Protected	Poor	Undrilled	-	Light Spear	3	8-12	0-16	

HYKSOS

The Hyksos (from the Egyptian *heqa khasewet*, "foreign rulers") were a people of Asiatic (possibly Amorite) origin who took over Lower (northern) Egypt in the mid-16th century BC. The traditional view of their accession to power is based on the history of Manetho, who wrote in Ptolemaic Egypt in the 3rd century BC. He recorded the Egyptian tradition that the Hyksos arrived as foreign invaders and took control of Lower Egypt by military force. Their supposed military success has in the past been attributed to their possession of the latest technology in the form of war chariots and composite bows. More recently it has been theorized that the Hyksos may in fact have arrived as nomadic settlers during a period of weakness under the Egyptian 13th dynasty, and taken over control gradually after perhaps being employed as soldiers and officials by the dynasty.

Whatever the truth, a *modus vivendi* was soon established between the Hyksos in Lower Egypt, ruling from Memphis, and the native Egyptian 17th dynasty in Upper (southern) Egypt, ruling from Thebes. This lasted until the final years of the 17th dynasty, when the Theban pharaohs launched an offensive against the Hyksos. The reconquest was completed by Ahmose I, the first pharaoh of the 18th century, who finally drove the Hyksos from Egypt c.1535.

This list covers Hyksos armies from c.1650 to c.1535 BC.

TROOP NOTES

We assume that retinue close fighters were armed with typical Amorite weaponry as depicted on Old Babylonian terracottas – javelins, bronze sickle sword and shield.

Hyksos Javelinman

HYKSOS STARTER ARMY		
Commander-in-Chief	1	Field Commander
Sub-commanders	2	2 x Troop Commander
Chariots	2 BGs	Each comprising 4 bases of chariots: Superior, Drilled Light Chariots – Bow
Retinue close fighters	4 BGs	Each comprising 8 bases of retinue close fighters: Average, Protected, Drilled Medium Foot – Light Spear, Swordsmen
Javelinmen	2 BGs	Each comprising 6 bases of javelinmen: Average, Unprotected, Undrilled Light Foot – Javelins, Light Spear
Archers	1 BG	8 bases of skirmishing archers: Average, Unprotected, Undrilled Light Foot – Bow
Slingers	1 BG	6 bases of slingers: Average, Unprotected, Undrilled Light Foot – Sling
Camp	1	Unfortified camp
Total	10 BGs	Camp, 8 mounted bases, 58 foot bases, 3 commanders

BUILDING A CUSTOMISED LIST USING OUR ARMY POINTS

Choose an army based on the maxima and minima in the list below. The following special instructions apply to this army:

• Commanders should be depicted in chariots.

HYKSOS									
Territory Types: Developed, Agricultural									
C-in-C		Inspired Commander/Field Commander/Troop Commander				80/50/35		1	
Sub-commanders		Field Commander				50		0-2	
		Troop Commander				35		0-3	
Troop name		Troop Type				Capabilities		Points per base	Bases per BG	Total bases
		Type	Armour	Quality	Training	Shooting	Close Combat			
Core Troops										
Chariots	Before 1590	Light Chariots	-	Superior	Drilled	Bow	-	18	4-6	0-6
	From 1590									4-16
Retinue close fighters with sickle sword or axe		Medium Foot	Protected	Average	Drilled	-	Light Spear, Swordsmen	7	6-8	16-60
Retinue archers		Medium Foot	Unprotected	Average	Drilled	Bow	-	6	6-8	0-8
Javelinmen		Medium Foot	Protected	Average	Undrilled	-	Light Spear	5	6-8	0-64 / 6-92
		Light Foot	Unprotected	Average	Undrilled	Javelins	Light Spear	4	6-8	0-32
Skirmishing archers		Light Foot	Unprotected	Average	Undrilled	Bow	-	5	6-8	0-16 / 6-32
Slingers		Light Foot	Unprotected	Average	Undrilled	Sling	-	4	6-8	0-16
Allies										
Egyptian vassals – Old or Middle Kingdom Egyptian										

MITANNI

Following the sack of Babylon by the Hittites c.1595 BC, the various Indo-Aryan Hurrian groupings in northern Mesopotamia were united under one dynasty as the Kingdom of Mitanni (or Hanigalbat). Its capital was Washshukanni. By the mid-15th century BC, Assyria had become a vassal state. At its greatest extent, in the early 14th century, the kingdom included modern south-east Turkey, northern Syria and northern Iraq.

Circa 1350, after Hittite intervention in a dynastic dispute, Mitanni became a buffer state between the Hittite Empire and Assyria, allied to the Hittites. Circa 1300 it became a vassal state of Assyria. Circa 1250 a rebellion against Assyria, with Hittite assistance, was crushed, part of the population was deported and an Assyrian governor was installed.

This list covers the armies of the Kingdom of Mitanni from 1595 to 1250 BC.

TROOP NOTES

The strength of Mitanni's armies was in it chariots, crewed by the noble *maryannu* class. The main weapon of these chariot warriors was the composite bow. Both warriors and drivers were well protected in suits of bronze scale or lamellar

Mitanni Spearman

armour, extending to the elbow and to the knee or below. The horses and the chariots themselves were also armoured. These styles were copied by other nations throughout Mesopotamia, Syria, Canaan and, to a lesser extent, Egypt.

The *maryannu* class formed a sort of feudal nobility, but the armour and weapons of royal *maryannu* at least were supplied by state armouries. We give the option of treating each battle group as drilled or undrilled.

Some, at least, of the infantry were equipped with swords and leather armour.

Mitanni chariot crew, by Angus McBride. Taken from Elite 40: New Kingdom Egypt.

MITANNI STARTER ARMY		
Commander-in-Chief	1	Field Commander
Sub-commanders	2	2 x Troop Commander
Chariots	5 BGs	Each comprising 4 bases of chariots: Superior, Undrilled Light Chariots – Bow
Spearmen and Archers	2 BGs	Each comprising 4 bases of spearmen: Average, Protected, Undrilled Medium Foot – Light Spear, Swordsmen, and 4 bases of archers: Average, Protected, Undrilled Medium Foot – Bow
Levy Javelinmen	1 BG	8 bases of levy javelinmen: Poor, Unprotected, Undrilled Light Foot – Javelins, Light Spear
Levy archers	1 BG	8 bases of levy archers: Poor, Unprotected, Undrilled Light Foot – Bow
Camp	1	Unfortified camp
Total	9 BGs	Camp, 20 mounted bases, 32 foot bases, 3 commanders

BUILDING A CUSTOMISED LIST USING OUR ARMY POINTS

Choose an army based on the maxima and minima in the list below. The following special instructions apply to this army:

- Commanders should be depicted in chariots.
- Spearmen and archers can be in mixed or separate battle groups.

Mitanni Levy Archer

MITANNI									
Territory Types: Agricultural, Hilly									
C-in-C	Inspired Commander/Field Commander/Troop Commander						80/50/35		1
Sub-commanders	Field Commander						50		0-2
	Troop Commander						35		0-3
Troop name	Troop Type				Capabilities		Points per base	Bases per BG	Total bases
	Type	Armour	Quality	Training	Shooting	Close Combat			
Core Troops									
Chariots	Light Chariots	-	Superior	Drilled	Bow	-	18	4-6	8-44
				Undrilled			17		
Spearmen	Medium Foot	Protected	Average	Drilled	-	Light Spear, Swordsmen	7	1/2 or all	8-24
				Undrilled			6		
	Medium Foot	Protected	Average	Drilled	-	Light Spear	6	6-8	
				Undrilled			5		
Archers	Medium Foot	Protected	Average	Drilled	Bow	-	7	1/2 or 0	8-24
				Undrilled			6		
	Medium Foot	Unprotected	Average	Drilled	Bow	-	6	6-8	
				Undrilled			5		
	Light Foot	Unprotected	Average	Drilled or Undrilled	Bow	-	5	6-8	
Levy foot	Medium Foot	Unprotected	Poor	Undrilled	-	Light Spear	2	6-8	6-24
	Light foot	Unprotected	Poor	Undrilled	Javelins	Light Spear	2		
	Light Foot	Unprotected	Poor	Undrilled	Bow	-	3		
Optional Troops									
Javelin skirmishers	Light foot	Unprotected	Average	Undrilled	Javelins	Light Spear	4	6-8	0-12
Levy dregs	Mob	Unprotected	Poor	Undrilled	-	-	2	8-12	0-12
Allies									
Nomad allies – Early Nomad									
Syro-Canaanite allies (Only before 1350)									
Hittite allies (Only from 1350) – Hittite Empire									

MITANNI ALLIES								
Allied commander		Field Commander/Troop Commander				40/25	1	
Troop name	Troop Type				Capabilities		Points per base	Bases per BG	Total bases
	Type	Armour	Quality	Training	Shooting	Close Combat			
Chariots	Light Chariots	-	Superior	Drilled	Bow	-	18	4-6	4-12
				Undrilled			17		
Spearmen	Medium Foot	Protected	Average	Drilled	-	Light Spear, Swordsmen	7	1/2 or all	0-8
				Undrilled			6		
	Medium Foot	Protected	Average	Drilled	-	Light Spear	6	6-8	
				Undrilled			5		
Archers	Medium Foot	Protected	Average	Drilled	Bow	-	7	1/2 or 0	0-8
				Undrilled			6		
	Medium Foot	Unprotected	Average	Drilled	Bow	-	6	6-8	0-8
				Undrilled			5		
	Light Foot	Unprotected	Average	Drilled or Undrilled	Bow	-	5	6-8	
Levy foot	Medium Foot	Unprotected	Poor	Undrilled	-	Light Spear	2	6-8	0-8
	Light foot	Unprotected	Poor	Undrilled	Javelins	Light Spear	2		
	Light Foot	Unprotected	Poor	Undrilled	Bow	-	3		

SYRO-CANAANITE

This list covers the armies of Canaan (the modern region from Gaza to Lebanon) and Syria from the early 16th century BC, following the upheavals consequent upon defeat by the Hittites, until 1100 BC.

The area was a patch-work of city states, and substantial armies had to be coalitions. Desert nomad raids, sometimes in substantial force, were a problem, as were the imperial ambitions of the great powers. Successful rulers managed to play the great powers off against each other. By the mid-14th century Egypt was in firm control of Canaan and southern Syria, with a number of Egyptian garrisons throughout the country. The city-states, however, were left to rule themselves, and even war amongst themselves, as long as the tribute continued to flow. Egyptian control collapsed following the Sea Peoples incursions of the late 13th and early 12th centuries.

Palestine came under the control of one such group, the Philistines, who came into conflict with the neighbouring Canaanite cites but gradually absorbed their culture. Their armies are covered by their own list.

TROOP NOTES

Chariotry was the pre-eminent arm and was very similar to Mitanni types in appearance (see above). Infantry was mostly lightly equipped and very much subordinate to the chariotry.

Ugarit, on the coast of northern Syria, was one of the larger Syro-Canaanite city states, and may have started using 3-crew chariots under Hittite influence. As the use of 3-crew chariots by the Hittites themselves is now in doubt, this option is mainly kept for compatibility with older interpretations.

Syro-Canaanite Chariot

SYRO-CANAANITE STARTER ARMY

Commander-in-Chief	1	Field Commander
Sub-commander	1	Troop Commander
Chariots	3 BGs	Each comprising 4 bases of chariots: Superior, Undrilled Light Chariots – Bow
Guard infantry	1 BG	6 bases of guard infantry: Superior, Protected, Drilled Medium Foot – Light Spear, Swordsmen
Sea Peoples mercenaries	1 BG	6 bases of Sea Peoples mercenaries: Average, Protected, Undrilled Medium Foot – Impact Foot, Swordsmen
Javelinmen	1 BG	6 bases of javelinmen: Average, Protected, Undrilled Medium Foot – Light Spear
Javelinmen	1 BG	6 bases of javelinmen: Average, Unprotected, Undrilled Light Foot – Javelins, Light Spear
Archers	1 BG	8 bases of archers: Average, Unprotected, Undrilled Light Foot – Bow
Syro-Canaanite allied commander	1	Troop Commander
Allied chariots	1 BG	4 bases of chariots: Superior, Undrilled Light Chariots – Bow
Allied javelinmen	1 BG	6 bases of javelinmen: Average, Unprotected, Undrilled Light Foot – Javelins, Light Spear
Camp	1	Unfortified camp
Total	10 BGs	Camp, 16 mounted bases, 38 foot bases, 3 commanders

BUILDING A CUSTOMISED LIST USING OUR ARMY POINTS

Choose an army based on the maxima and minima in the list below. The following special instructions apply to this army:

- Commanders should be depicted in chariots.
- A Syro-Canaanite allied commander's contingent must conform to the Syro-Canaanite allies list below, but the troops in the contingent are deducted from the minima and maxima in the main list.
- The main army (excluding allied contingents) cannot include more than 16 chariot bases (excluding commanders).

- Ugaritic heavy chariots can only be used in the main army if the C-in-C is Ugaritic, otherwise must be under the command of an Ugaritic allied commander. An Ugaritic allied commander cannot be used if the C-in-C is Ugaritic. Only one Ugaritic allied commander can be used.
- Egyptians and Mitanni cannot be used together.
- Ugaritic heavy chariots cannot be used with Egyptian allies.

Sea Peoples Mercenary

SYRO-CANAANITE

Territory Types: Developed, Agricultural, Hilly

C-in-C		Inspired Commander/Field Commander/Troop Commander					80/50/35		1	
Sub-commanders		Field Commander/Troop Commander					50/35		0-2	
Syro-Canaanite allied commanders		Field Commander/Troop Commander					40/25		0-2	

Troop name		Troop Type				Capabilities		Points per base	Bases per BG	Total bases	
		Type	Armour	Quality	Training	Shooting	Close Combat				
Core Troops											
Chariots	Any	Light Chariots	-	Superior	Undrilled	Bow	-	17	4-6	0-36	8-36
3-crew chariots	Only Ugaritic from 1275	Heavy Chariots	-	Superior	Undrilled	Bow	-	20	4-6	0-16	
Javelinmen		Medium Foot	Protected	Average	Undrilled	-	Light Spear	5	6-8	6-16	8-48
		Medium Foot	Unprotected	Average	Undrilled	-	Light Spear	4	6-8	6-48	
		Light Foot	Unprotected	Average	Undrilled	Javelins	Light Spear	4	6-8		
		Medium Foot	Unprotected	Poor	Undrilled	-	Light Spear	2	6-8	0-16	
		Light Foot	Unprotected	Poor	Undrilled	Javelins	Light Spear	2	6-8		
Archers		Medium Foot	Unprotected	Average	Undrilled	Bow	-	5	6-8	6-32	6-32
		Light Foot	Unprotected	Average	Undrilled	Bow	-	5	6-8		
		Medium Foot	Unprotected	Poor	Undrilled	Bow	-	3	6-8	0-16	
		Light Foot	Unprotected	Poor	Undrilled	Bow	-	3	6-8		
Optional Troops											
Guard infantry		Medium Foot	Protected	Superior	Drilled	-	Light spear, Swordsmen	9	4-6	0-6	
		Medium Foot	Unprotected	Superior	Drilled	Bow	-	7	4-6		
Slingers		Light Foot	Unprotected	Average	Undrilled	Sling	-	4	6-8	0-8	
Sea Peoples mercenaries	Only from 1207	Medium Foot	Protected	Average	Undrilled	-	Impact Foot, Swordsmen	7	4-6	0-6	
Allies											
Egyptian allies – New Kingdom Egyptian											
Mitanni allies (Only before 1350)											

SYRO-CANAANITE ALLIES

Allied commander		Field Commander/Troop Commander					40/25		1	
Troop name		**Troop Type**				**Capabilities**		**Points per base**	**Bases per BG**	**Total bases**
		Type	Armour	Quality	Training	Shooting	Close Combat			
Chariots	Any	Light Chariots	-	Superior	Undrilled	Bow	-	17	4-6	0-12 / 4-12
3-crew chariots	Only Ugaritic from 1275	Heavy Chariots	-	Superior	Undrilled	Bow	-	20	4-6	0-12
Javelinmen		Medium Foot	Protected	Average	Undrilled	-	Light Spear	5	6	0-6
		Medium Foot	Unprotected	Average	Undrilled	-	Light Spear	4	6-8	6-16 / 6-16
		Light Foot	Unprotected	Average	Undrilled	Javelins	Light Spear	4	6-8	
		Medium Foot	Unprotected	Poor	Undrilled	-	Light Spear	2	6	0-6
		Light Foot	Unprotected	Poor	Undrilled	Javelins	Light Spear	2	6	
Archers		Medium Foot	Unprotected	Average	Undrilled	Bow	-	5	6-8	0-12 / 0-12
		Light Foot	Unprotected	Average	Undrilled	Bow	-	5	6-8	
		Medium Foot	Unprotected	Poor	Undrilled	Bow	-	3	6	0-6
		Light Foot	Unprotected	Poor	Undrilled	Bow	-	3	6	

Canaanite chariot crew and Egyptian infantry, by Angus McBride. Taken from Elite 40: New Kingdom Egypt.

NEW KINGDOM EGYPTIAN

The period known as the New Kingdom, from 1550 to 1069 BC, marked the zenith of Egyptian power, under the 18th, 19th and 20th dynasties.

The first pharaoh of the 18th dynasty, Ahmose I, had driven the Hyksos out of Lower (northern) Egypt by 1535. Egyptian armies moved back into Nubia and by the end of the reign of Thutmose I (1504–1492) the frontier had been advanced to the Fourth Cataract of the Nile. In the Levant also, Egyptian control was re-established and extended. Following the campaigns of Thutmose III (1479–1425) which extended north as far as the Kingdom of Mitanni, the Egyptian Empire reached its greatest extent, from southern Syria to the Fourth Cataract in Nubia.

During the later 18th dynasty, the Hittites expanded their influence into Syria and Palestine. The early 19th dynasty pharaohs Seti I (1290–1279) and Ramesses II (1279–1213) came into conflict with them. At Kadesh in Syria in 1274, Ramesses's army was ambushed by the Hittites under Muwatalli II, but managed to fight them to a stalemate, both sides afterwards claiming victory. Following this, Hittite control was confirmed in Syria, while Egypt retained Canaan.

In the reign of Ramesses III (1183–1152), the second pharaoh of the 20th dynasty, Egypt suffered several attacks from large armies of Libyans and

Sea Peoples. These were defeated, but not without heavy losses and enormous strain on the economy. Following the death of Ramesses III, the rest of the dynasty was characterised by internecine strife, droughts, official corruption and civil unrest. The frontiers contracted, with the loss of Nubia and Canaan, much of the latter coming under the control of the Philistines, survivors of the Sea Peoples' defeat who were either settled in Canaan by Ramesses III or took the territory by force. Even before the death of the last pharaoh of the dynasty, Ramesses XI, in 1069, Upper (southern) Egypt was being ruled by the High Priests of Amun at Thebes, while Lower Egypt was under the control of Smendes (Nesbanebdjed) who subsequently founded the 21st dynasty. This ushered in the Third Intermediate Period.

This list covers the armies of the 18th, 19th and 20th dynasties from 1550 to 1069 BC.

THE BATTLE OF KADESH

This battle is one of the best documented in the chariot period. It was fought near the strategically important city of Kadesh in Syria between the Egyptian army of King Ramesses II and the Hittite army of Muwatalli II. The most commonly accepted date for the battle (depending on which chronology is used) is 1274 BC.

The Egyptian army was advancing in an attempt to capture Kadesh. The Hittites used local Bedouin to feed Ramesses false information, leading him to believe that the Hittites were many miles

Ramesses in his chariot

Egyptian chariot training, by Brian Delf. Taken from New Vanguard 119: Bronze Age War Chariots.

away. In fact the Hittite army was close at hand, hidden behind "Old Kadesh" near Kadesh. In an attempt to capture Kadesh before the Hittites could arrive, Ramesses forced marched his army, so that it arrived in column of divisions with large gaps in between. The regular Egyptian troops were in four divisions, from front to rear Amun, Re (P're), Ptah and Seth (Suteh). There was also an advance guard called Ne'arin which may have been allied troops from Amurru, or a detachment of Egyptian troops.

Ramesses had arrived at Kadesh with the Amun division, and begun to make camp, when two new Hittite spies were captured and under torture revealed the proximity of the Hittite army. Ramesses sent messengers to hasten the march of his rear divisions. Almost immediately, however, the main Hittite chariot force of 2,500 chariots,

each carrying a chariot runner in addition to its normal two crewmen, swept down on the Re division. This was in the process of fording the River Orontes, and was immediately put to flight. The Hittites then pursued into the half-completed Egyptian camp, where King Ramesses attempted to rally some resistance. Fortunately the Hittite troops started to loot the camp and were in some disorder, so that Ramesses was able to hold out until the Ne'arin advance guard returned and charged the Hittite chariots in the rear.

Egyptian Standard Bearer

The Battle of Qadesh, by Adam Hook. Taken from Warrior 120: Hittite Warrior.

Muwatalli then ordered in his reserve chariots, numbering 1,000, but the Ne'arin managed to cut their way through to join Ramesses, who then went on the offensive. With the arrival of the Ptah division, the Egyptians were eventually able to drive the Hittites back across the river, many of them being drowned. Muwatalli remained on the far side of the river throughout the battle, with a huge number of infantry, who were not committed. The Egyptian Seth division failed to arrive until after the fighting was over.

The next day there was some desultory fighting, ending in Muwatalli offering Ramesses a truce. This allowed the Egyptian army to withdraw to Egypt. Afterwards both sides claimed victory, but the Hittites retained their territorial gains.

TROOP NOTES

Hand-to-hand weapons were not standardised within close-fighter units, which were armed with a mixture of hand axes, khopesh (sickle swords), mace-axes and spear-swords. We treat them as equivalent to Swordsmen.

Egyptian Close Fighter

Egyptian Officer

NEW KINGDOM EGYPTIAN STARTER ARMY		
Commander-in-Chief	1	Field Commander
Sub-commander	2	2 x Troop Commander
Egyptian chariots	3 BGs	Each comprising 4 bases of Egyptian chariots: Superior, Drilled Light Chariots – Bow
Canaanite chariots	1 BG	4 bases of Canaanite chariots: Superior, Undrilled Light Chariots – Bow
Close fighters	2 BGs	Each comprising 6 bases of close fighters: Average, Protected, Drilled Medium Foot – Light Spear, Swordsmen
Archers	2 BGs	Each comprising 6 bases of archers: Average, Unprotected, Drilled Medium Foot – Bow
Nubian archers	1 BG	8 bases of Nubian archers: Average, Unprotected, Undrilled, Light Foot – Bow
Camp	1	Unfortified camp
Total	9 BGs	Camp, 16 mounted bases, 32 foot bases, 3 commanders

BUILDING A CUSTOMISED LIST USING OUR ARMY POINTS

Choose an army based on the maxima and minima in the list below. The following special instructions apply to this army:

- Commanders should be depicted in chariots.
- Close fighters can interpenetrate archers and vice versa.

The chariot of Ramesses II, 1288 BC, by Angus McBride. Taken from Men-at-Arms 109: **Ancient Armies of the Middle East.**

NEW KINGDOM EGYPTIAN

Territory Types: Developed, Agricultural

C-in-C		Inspired Commander/Field Commander/Troop Commander					80/50/35		1	
Sub-commanders		Field Commander					50		0-2	
		Troop Commander					35		0-3	
Troop name		**Troop Type**				**Capabilities**		**Points per base**	**Bases per BG**	**Total bases**
		Type	Armour	Quality	Training	Shooting	Close Combat			
Core Troops										
Chariots		Light Chariots	-	Superior	Drilled	Bow	-	18	4-6	6-26
Close fighters		Medium Foot	Protected	Average	Drilled	-	Light Spear, Swordsmen	7	6-8	6-36
Archers		Medium Foot	Unprotected	Average	Drilled	Bow	-	6	6-8	12-48
Optional Troops										
Egyptian guardsmen		Heavy Foot	Armoured	Superior	Drilled	-	Light Spear, Swordsmen	12	4	0-4
			Protected					9		
Canaanite or Syrian chariots	Only from 1450 to 1150	Light Chariots	-	Superior	Undrilled	Bow	-	17	4-6	0-6
Bedouin, Canaanite, Libyan or Syrian javelinmen		Medium Foot	Protected	Average	Undrilled	-	Light spear	5	6-8	0-8
			Unprotected					4	6-8	
		Light Foot	Unprotected	Average	Undrilled	Javelins	Light Spear	4	6-8	0-16
Canaanite or Syrian archers		Light Foot	Unprotected	Average	Undrilled	Bow	-	5	6-8	
Nubian archers		Light Foot	Unprotected	Superior	Undrilled	Bow	-	6	6-8	0-8
				Average				5		
Sherden guardsmen	Only from 1279	Heavy Foot	Armoured	Superior	Drilled	-	Impact Foot, Swordsmen	13	4	0-4
			Protected					10		
Sherden or other Sea Peoples swordsmen	Only from 1200	Medium Foot	Protected	Average	Undrilled	-	Impact Foot, Swordsmen	7	8-12	0-24
Libyan swordsmen	Only from 1200	Medium Foot	Unprotected	Average	Undrilled	-	Impact Foot, Swordsmen	6	8-12	0-24
Fortified Camp								24		0-1

NEW KINGDOM EGYPTIAN ALLIES

Allied commander		Field Commander/Troop Commander					40/25		1	
Troop name		**Troop Type**				**Capabilities**		**Points per base**	**Bases per BG**	**Total bases**
		Type	Armour	Quality	Training	Shooting	Close Combat			
Chariots		Light Chariots	-	Superior	Drilled	Bow	-	18	4-6	4-8
Close fighters		Medium Foot	Protected	Average	Drilled	-	Light Spear, Swordsmen	7	4-8	4-8
Archers		Medium Foot	Unprotected	Average	Drilled	Bow	-	6	4-8	4-12
Sherden or other Sea Peoples swordsmen	Only from 1200	Medium Foot	Protected	Average	Undrilled	-	Impact Foot, Swordsmen	7	6-8	0-8
Libyan swordsmen		Medium Foot	Unprotected	Average	Undrilled	-	Impact Foot, Swordsmen	6	4-6	0-6

LATER MINOAN OR EARLY MYCENAEAN

Minoan civilisation flourished on Crete from the 3rd millenium BC until Crete was taken over by the Mycenaeans in the mid-15th century BC. Mycenaean civilisation, which borrowed much from Minoan culture, ruled Greece from the early 16th century until it collapsed in the upheavals of the early 12th century.

This list covers Minoan armies from c.1600 to c.1450 BC, and Mycenaean armies from c.1600 to c.1250. The Later Mycenaean period is covered by its own list.

TROOP NOTES

Although most chariots carried only two crewmen, the very heavy and relatively inflexible bronze plate armour (Dendra panoply) of chariot warriors in this period, the use of a long spear as main weapon, and the strengthened chariot structure compared with Near-Eastern types, suggest that they were intended primarily for close combat and should be classified as Heavy Chariots.

Spearmen carried very long spears wielded in both hands and very large "tower" or "figure of eight" ox-hide body shields hung from a shoulder strap.

Later Minoan Spearman

LATER MINOAN OR EARLY MYCENAEAN STARTER ARMY		
Commander-in-Chief	1	Field Commander
Sub-commander	2	2 x Troop Commander
Chariots	2 BGs	Each comprising 4 bases of chariots: Superior, Drilled Heavy Chariots – Light Spear
Spearmen and archers	4 BGs	Each comprising 6 bases of spearmen: Average, Protected, Drilled Heavy Foot – Defensive Spearmen, and 3 bases of supporting archers: Average, Unprotected, Drilled Light Foot – Bow
Light Infantry	1 BG	6 bases of light infantry: Average, Protected, Drilled Medium Foot – Light Spear
Separately deployed archers	1 BG	6 bases of separately deployed archers: Average, Unprotected, Drilled Light Foot – Bow
Slingers	1 BG	6 bases of slingers: Average, Unprotected, Drilled Light Foot – Sling
Camp	1	Unfortified camp
Total	9 BGs	Camp, 8 mounted bases, 54 foot bases, 3 commanders

Early Mycenaean infantry, c.1500 BC, by Angus McBride. Taken from Elite 130: The Mycenaeans c.1650–1100 BC.

BUILDING A CUSTOMISED LIST USING OUR ARMY POINTS

Choose an army based on the maxima and minima in the list below. The following special instructions apply to this army:

- Commanders should be depicted in chariots.

LATER MINOAN OR EARLY MYCENAEAN									
Territory Types: Agricultural, Hilly									
C-in-C	Inspired Commander/Field Commander/Troop Commander						80/50/35	1	
Sub-commanders	Field Commander						50	0-2	
	Troop Commander						35	0-3	
Troop name	Troop Type				Capabilities		Points per base	Bases per BG	Total bases
	Type	Armour	Quality	Training	Shooting	Close Combat			
Core Troops									
Chariots	Heavy Chariots	-	Superior	Drilled	-	Light Spear	20	4-6	6-24
Spearmen	Heavy Foot	Protected	Average	Drilled	-	Defensive Spearmen	7	2/3 or all	12-60
Supporting archers	Light Foot	Unprotected	Average	Drilled	Bow	-	5	1/3 or 0	6-9
Separately deployed archers	Light Foot	Unprotected	Average	Drilled or Undrilled	Bow	-	5	6-8	6-30
	Medium Foot	Unprotected	Average	Drilled	Bow	-	6	6-8	0-12
				Undrilled			5		
Optional Troops									
Light infantry	Medium Foot	Protected	Average	Drilled	-	Light Spear	6	6-8	0-12
	Medium Foot	Unprotected	Average	Drilled	-	Light Spear, Swordsmen	6		
Slingers	Light Foot	Unprotected	Average	Undrilled	Sling	-	4	6-8	0-8
Javelinmen	Light Foot	Unprotected	Average	Undrilled	Javelins	Light Spear	4	6-8	0-16

Early Mycenaean chariot, by Angus McBride. Taken from Elite 130: The Mycenaeans c.1650–1100 BC.

HITTITE EMPIRE

The Hittite Old Kingdom arose in the 17th century BC as a result of the migration of the Indo-European Hittites into eastern central Anatolia (in modern Turkey) and their acquisition of the Hattian city of Hattusa as their capital. The invaders borrowed much of their culture from the non-Indo-European Hattians. After a period of expansion, culminating in the sack of Babylon by Mursili I in 1595, the over-stretched kingdom collapsed into anarchy. The Hurrians took advantage of the chaos to set up states in Mitanni (see page 19) and Kizzuwatna (later Cilicia). From then until the end of the so-called Middle Kingdom, the Hittite kingdom contracted to its core territory.

The Hittite New Kingdom begins with the reign of Tudhaliya I at the end of the 15th century

BC. In alliance with Kizzuwatna, he defeated Hurrian Aleppo and Mitanni and expanded westwards at the expense of the Luwian state of Arzawa. Following his death the enemies of the Hittites counterattacked and even sacked Hattusa.

Suppiluliuma I restored the power of the kingdom, conquering Aleppo and Carchemish, and reducing Mitanni to vassal status c.1350 under his son-in-law Shattiwaza. In the later 14th century, Mursili II expanded the Hittite Empire westwards.

In the early 13th century, Egyptian expansion into Syria threatened Hittite influence and

Hittite Standard Bearer

Hittite chariot, by Angus McBride. Taken from Elite 40: New Kingdom Egypt.

trade, resulting in the Battle of Kadesh c.1274 between the Hittites under Muwatalli II and the Egyptians under Ramesses II (see page 26). This was a draw, but confirmed Syria as a Hittite protectorate, while Egypt retained control of Canaan.

Following the death of Muwatalli II the Empire began to decline again. The Sea Peoples upheavals of the late 13th and early 12th centuries weakened it further. c.1180 it succumbed to combined attack by the Gasgans, Bryges (Phrygians) and Luwians, and Hattusa was destroyed.

This list covers the armies of the Hittite New Kingdom from c.1400 to c.1180 BC.

TROOP NOTES

Current thinking is that Hittite chariots were primarily bow-armed like other contemporary Near Eastern chariotry. We allow either the current or the old interpretation to be used. Egyptian reliefs of the battle of Kadesh show Hittite chariots apparently with three crew. We therefore allow this as an option. However, it is now thought more likely that the third man represents a chariot runner being given a lift for speed when the Hittite chariots burst from ambush.

Chariots from the West Anatolian vassal states are more likely to have been influenced by Aegean tactics and are therefore less likely to have been bow armed.

Egyptian infantry close fighters are depicted conventionally in the Kadesh reliefs with spear in one hand, sword in the other and shield slung on their backs. Hittite infantry are depicted in exactly the same way except that shields are not depicted. We know from other sources that at least some Hittite infantry did carry shields, and it is entirely possible that they are not depicted in the Kadesh reliefs due to lack of an Egyptian artistic convention for rendering their differently shaped shields. It is quite likely, therefore, that Hittite infantry fought in a similar fashion to Egyptian close fighters, giving a classification of Medium Foot, Protected, Light Spear, Swordsmen. We follow this view rather than older interpretations, but retain the old interpretation as an option for those spearmen depicted as unshielded. An army can include both types.

HITTITE EMPIRE STARTER ARMY		
Commander-in-Chief	1	Field Commander
Sub-commander	2	2 x Troop Commander
Hittite, Arzawan, Masan or Pitassan chariots	3 BGs	Each comprising 4 bases of Hittite, Arzawan, Masan or Pitassan chariots: Superior, Drilled Light Chariots – Bow
Other Anatolian chariots	1 BG	4 bases of other Anatolian chariots: Superior, Undrilled Light Chariots – Bow
Hittite spearmen	2 BGs	Each comprising 8 bases of Hittite spearmen: Average, Protected, Drilled Medium Foot – Light Spear, Swordsmen
Anatolian javelinmen	1 BG	6 bases of Anatolian javelinmen: Average, Unprotected, Undrilled Light Foot – Javelins, Light Spear
Anatolian archers	1 BG	6 bases of Anatolian archers: Average, Unprotected, Undrilled Light Foot – Bow
Anatolian slingers	1 BG	6 bases of Anatolian slingers: Average, Unprotected, Undrilled Light Foot – Sling
Camp	1	Unfortified camp
Total	9 BGs	Camp, 16 mounted bases, 34 foot bases, 3 commanders

BUILDING A CUSTOMISED LIST USING OUR ARMY POINTS

Choose an army based on the maxima and minima in the list below. The following special instructions apply to this army:

- Commanders should be depicted in chariots.

- If any Hittite, Arzawan, Masan or Pitassan chariots have Bow capability, all must.
- Minima marked * apply only if any Syro-Canaanite troops are used.

Hittite Spearman

Buyukkale, citadel of Hattusha, late 13th century BC, by Brian Delf. Taken from Fortress 73: Hittite Fortifications c.1650–700 BC.

HITTITE EMPIRE

Territory Types: Agricultural, Hilly, Mountains

C-in-C		Inspired Commander/Field Commander/Troop Commander					80/50/35		1	
Sub-commanders		Field Commander					50		0-2	
		Troop Commander					35		0-3	

Troop name		Troop Type				Capabilities		Points per base	Bases per BG	Total bases
		Type	Armour	Quality	Training	Shooting	Close Combat			
Core Troops										
Hittite, Arzawan, Masan or Pitassan chariots	Any date	Light Chariots	-	Superior	Drilled	-	Bow	18	4-6	6-20
		Light Chariots	-	Superior	Drilled	-	Light Spear	16	4-6	
	Only from 1275	Heavy Chariots	-	Superior	Drilled	-	Bow	22	4-6	
		Heavy Chariots	-	Superior	Drilled	-	Light Spear	20	4-6	
Other Anatolian or Gasgan chariots		Light Chariots	-	Superior	Undrilled	-	Light Spear	15	4-6	4-8
				Average				11		
		Light Chariots	-	Superior	Undrilled	-	Bow	17	4-6	
				Average				13		
Hittite spearmen		Medium Foot	Protected	Average	Drilled	-	Light Spear, Swordsmen	7	6-8	8-36
		Medium Foot	Unprotected	Average	Drilled	-	Defensive Spearmen	6	6-8	
Optional Troops										
Syro-Canaanite chariots		Light Chariots	-	Superior	Undrilled	Bow	-	17	4-6	*4-12
3-crew Ugaritic chariots	Only from 1275	Heavy Chariots	-	Superior	Undrilled	Bow	-	20	4	0-4
Anatolian, Syro-Canaanite or Bedouin spearmen/javelinmen with shields		Medium Foot	Protected	Average	Undrilled	-	Light Spear	5	6-8	0-12
Syro-Canaanite spearmen without shields		Medium Foot	Unprotected	Average	Undrilled	-	Light Spear	4	8-12	*8-24
				Poor				2		
Anatolian or Bedouin archers		Light Foot	Unprotected	Average	Undrilled	Bow	-	5	6-8	0-8
				Poor				3		
Syro-Canaanite archers		Light Foot	Unprotected	Average	Undrilled	Bow	-	5	6-8	*6-12
				Poor				3		
		Medium Foot	Unprotected	Average	Undrilled	Bow	-	5	6-8	
				Poor				3		
Anatolian or Bedouin slingers		Light Foot	Unprotected	Average	Undrilled	Sling	-	4	6-8	0-8
				Poor				2		
Anatolian, Syro-Canaanite or Bedouin skirmishing javelinmen		Light Foot	Unprotected	Average	Undrilled	Javelins	Light Spear	4	6-8	0-8
				Poor				2		
Gasgan foot		Medium Foot	Protected	Average	Undrilled	-	Impact Foot, Swordsmen	7	6-12	0-12
Poor quality levies		Mob	Unprotected	Poor	Undrilled	-	-	2	8-12	0-12
Allies										
Mitanni vassal allies										

HITTITE EMPIRE ALLIES									
Allied commander		Field Commander/Troop Commander					40/25		1
Troop name		Troop Type				Capabilities		Points per base	Bases per BG	Total bases
		Type	Armour	Quality	Training	Shooting	Close Combat			
Hittite, Arzawan, Masan or Pitassan chariots	Any date	Light Chariots	-	Superior	Drilled	-	Bow	18	4-6	4-8
		Light Chariots	-	Superior	Drilled	-	Light Spear	16	4-6	
	Only from 1275	Heavy Chariots	-	Superior	Drilled	-	Bow	22	4-6	
		Heavy Chariots	-	Superior	Drilled	-	Light Spear	20	4-6	
Hittite spearmen		Medium Foot	Protected	Average	Drilled		Light Spear, Swordsmen	7	6-8	0-12
		Medium Foot	Unprotected	Average	Drilled		Defensive Spearmen	6	6-8	
Skirmishers		Light Foot	Unprotected	Average	Undrilled	Bow	-	5	4-6	0-6
		Light Foot	Unprotected	Average	Undrilled	Javelins	Light spear	4	4-6	
		Light Foot	Unprotected	Average	Undrilled	Sling	-	4	4-6	

MIDDLE OR EARLY NEO-ASSYRIAN

In the 15th century BC, Assyria (in modern northern Iraq) was conquered by the Kingdom of Mitanni and reduced to vassal status. However, following the reduction of Mitanni to vassal status by the Hittites in the mid-14th century, Assyria was able to reassert its independence under Ashur-uballit I (1365–1330) and start to expand once more, including intervening in Babylonian dynastic disputes. Mitanni was conquered and reduced to vassal status under Adad-nirari I (1307–1275). Shalmaneser I (1274–1245) defeated a Mitanni revolt supported by the Hittites, and subjected the rump of Mitanni to direct rule under an Assyrian governor. He also conquered several cities from the Hittites. Tukulti-Ninurta I (1244–1208) inflicted a severe defeat on the Hittites and also captured Babylon although it subsequently successfully revolted. However, under his son Ashur-nadin-apli (1207–1204) Assyria lost much of its power, and internecine strife marked the next few reigns. During the reigns of the Babylonian kings Melishipak II (1185–1170)

and Marduk-apal-iddin I (1170–1157) Assyria was forced to accept tributary status.

Tiglath-Pileser I (1115–1076) was the next great Assyrian conqueror, expanding the kingdom's power in all directions, and campaigning as far as the Mediterranean. Following his reign, however, Assyrian power once more declined.

This decline ended with the accession of Adad-nirari II (912–891) the first king of the Neo-Assyrian period. He, his son Tukulti-Ninurta II (891–884), his grandson Ashur-nasir-pal II (884–859) and great-grandson Shalmaneser III (859–824) relentlessly and successfully campaigned against the surrounding states – although the latter's advance into Syria was halted by a coalition of several Aramaean and Neo-Hittite kingdoms with Israel at Qarqar in 853. As in previous periods of Assyrian

Tribal Levy Slinger

expansion, however, though tribute was exacted from defeated foes, their territories were not consolidated into a formal empire. There followed a period of relative decline, under weaker rulers – apart from Adad-nirari III (810–782), who expanded Assyrian influence in Syria – until the accession of Tiglath-Pileser III in 745.

This list covers the armies of Assyria from 1365 to 745 BC.

TROOP NOTES

In the early part of the period, chariots had two horses and two crewmen. From the early 9th century some chariots were heavier, with three crewmen and three or four horses. At the same time, cavalry started to come into use.

Hupshu were peasant conscripts. Asharittu were better equipped and trained "for a fight to the finish".

Ashurnasirpal II besieging a city, 9th century BC, by Angus McBride. Taken from Elite 39: The Ancient Assyrians.

EARLY NEO-ASSYRIAN STARTER ARMY		
Commander-in-Chief	1	Field Commander
Sub-commander	2	2 x Troop Commander
Heavy chariots	1 BG	4 bases of heavy chariots: Superior, Drilled Heavy Chariots – Bow
Light chariots	2 BGs	Each comprising 4 bases of light chariots: Superior, Drilled Light Chariots – Bow
Cavalry	1 BG	4 bases of cavalry: Average, Protected, Drilled Cavalry – 2 Light Spear, Swordsmen and 2 Bow, Swordsmen
Asharittu	2 BGs	Each comprising 4 bases of spearmen: Average, Protected, Drilled Medium Foot – Light Spear, Swordsmen, and 4 bases of archers: Average, Protected, Drilled Medium Foot – Bow
Hupshu	1 BG	4 bases of spearmen: Average, Protected, Undrilled Medium Foot – Light Spear, and 4 bases of archers: Average, Protected, Undrilled Medium Foot – Bow
Tribal levy archers	1 BG	8 bases of tribal levy archers: Poor, Unprotected, Undrilled Light Foot – Bow
Tribal levy slingers	1 BG	6 bases of tribal levy slingers: Poor, Unprotected, Undrilled Light Foot – Sling
Tribal levy javelinmen	1 BG	6 bases of tribal levy javelinmen: Poor, Unprotected, Undrilled Light Foot – Javelins, Light Spear
Camp	1	Unfortified camp
Total	10 BGs	Camp, 16 mounted bases, 44 foot bases, 3 commanders

BUILDING A CUSTOMISED LIST USING OUR ARMY POINTS

Choose an army based on the maxima and minima in the list below. The following special instructions apply to this army:

- Commanders should be depicted in chariots.

MIDDLE OR EARLY NEO-ASSYRIAN

Territory Types: Agricultural, Developed, Hilly

C-in-C		Inspired Commander/Field Commander/Troop Commander					80/50/35		1	
Sub-commanders		Field Commander					50		0-2	
		Troop Commander					35		0-3	
Troop name		Troop Type				Capabilities		Points per base	Bases per BG	Total bases
		Type	Armour	Quality	Training	Shooting	Close Combat			
Core Troops										
Chariots	Any date	Light Chariots	-	Superior	Drilled	Bow	-	18	4-6	4-24 / 8-24
	Only from 890	Heavy Chariots	-	Superior	Drilled	Bow	-	22	4-6	4-12
Cavalry	Only from 890	Cavalry	Protected	Average	Drilled	-	Light Spear, Swordsmen	10	1/2 / 4-6	0-12
		Cavalry	Protected	Average	Drilled	Bow	Swordsmen	12	1/2	
Asharittu		Medium Foot	Protected	Average	Drilled	-	Light Spear, Swordsmen	7	1/2 / 6-8	8-32
		Medium Foot	Protected	Average	Drilled	Bow	-	7	1/2	
Hupshu		Medium Foot	Protected	Average	Undrilled	-	Light Spear	5	1/2 / 6-8	0-64
		Medium Foot	Protected	Average	Undrilled	Bow	-	6	1/2	
		Medium Foot	Protected	Poor	Undrilled	-	Light Spear	3	1/2 / 8-10	
		Medium Foot	Protected	Poor	Undrilled	Bow	-	4	1/2	
Tribal levies		Light Foot	Unprotected / Poor	Average	Undrilled	Bow	-	5 / 3	6-8	0-24 / 0-24
		Light Foot	Unprotected / Poor	Average	Undrilled	Sling	-	4 / 2	6-8	0-8
		Light Foot	Unprotected / Poor	Average	Undrilled	Javelins	Light Spear	4 / 2	4-6	0-6
Optional Troops										
Levy dregs		Mob	Unprotected	Poor	Undrilled	-	-	2	8-12	0-12
Fortified camp								24		0-1
Allies										
Neo-Hittite and Aramaean allies (Only from 890)										

LATER MYCENAEAN OR TROJAN

This list covers Mycenaean armies from the mid-13th century until the early 12th century BC. It also covers Trojan armies of the Trojan War.

TROOP NOTES

A change to lighter chariot types and more lightly equipped crew in the mid-13th century BC suggests a change in chariot tactics.

Likewise there appears to have been a change of infantry equipment from long spears and very large body shields to shorter spears, smaller round shields and body armour.

In the Iliad, some infantry (Nestor's) still appear to use the old fighting style.

Dismounted Charioteer

Later Mycenaean spearmen, c.1250–1200 BC, by Angus McBride. Taken from Elite 130: The Mycenaeans *c.1650–1100 BC.*

LATER MYCENAEAN STARTER ARMY		
Commander-in-Chief	1	Field Commander
Sub-commander	2	2 x Troop Commander
Chariots	3 BGs	Each comprising 4 bases of chariots: Superior, Undrilled Light Chariots – Light Spear
Spearmen	2 BGs	Each comprising 6 bases of spearmen: Average, Armoured, Undrilled Medium Foot – Offensive Spearmen
Spearmen	2 BGs	Each comprising 8 bases of spearmen: Average, Protected, Undrilled Medium Foot – Offensive Spearmen
Javelinmen	1 BG	6 bases of javelinmen: Average, Unprotected, Undrilled Light Foot – Javelins, Light Spear
Archers	1 BG	6 bases of archers: Average, Unprotected, Undrilled Light Foot – Bow
Slingers	1 BG	6 bases of slingers: Average, Unprotected, Undrilled Light Foot – Sling
Camp	1	Unfortified camp
Total	10 BGs	Camp, 12 mounted bases, 46 foot bases, 3 commanders

BUILDING A CUSTOMISED LIST USING OUR ARMY POINTS

Choose an army based on the maxima and minima in the list below. The following special instructions apply to this army:

- Commanders should be depicted in chariots.
- Chariots can always dismount as Medium Foot, Armoured, Superior, Undrilled, Offensive Spearmen.

Myrmidon

LATER MYCENAEAN OR TROJAN

Territory Types: Agricultural, Hilly

Troop name	Troop Type				Capabilities		Points per base	Bases per BG	Total bases
C-in-C	Inspired Commander/Field Commander/Troop Commander						80/50/35		1
Sub-commanders	Field Commander						50		0-2
	Troop Commander						35		0 3
	Type	Armour	Quality	Training	Shooting	Close Combat			
Core Troops									
Chariots	Light Chariots	-	Superior	Undrilled	-	Light Spear	15	4-6	6-30
Spearmen	Medium Foot	Armoured	Average	Undrilled	-	Offensive Spearmen	9	6-8	0-12 — 12-66
	Medium Foot	Protected	Average	Undrilled	-	Offensive Spearmen	7	6-8	0-60
Javelinmen	Light foot	Unprotected	Average	Undrilled	Javelins	Light Spear	4	6-8	6-18
Archers	Light Foot	Unprotected	Average	Undrilled	Bow	-	5	6-8	6-12
	Medium Foot	Unprotected	Average	Undrilled	Bow	-	5	6-8	
Optional Troops									
Cavalry	Cavalry	Armoured	Average	Undrilled	-	Light Spear	10	4-6	0-6
		Protected					7		
Slingers	Light Foot	Unprotected	Average	Undrilled	Sling	-	4	6-8	0-8
Fortified Camp							24		0-1
Special Campaigns									
Only Achaians in the Trojan War									
Achilles's Myrmidons	Medium Foot	Armoured	Superior	Undrilled	-	Impact Foot, Swordsmen	12	4-6	0-6
		Protected					9		
Nestor's spearmen and supporting archers	Heavy Foot	Protected	Average	Drilled	-	Defensive Spearmen	7	2/3 or all	0-18
	Light Foot	Unprotected	Average	Drilled	Bow	-	5	1/3 or 0	6-9
Only Trojans in the Trojan War									
Sarpedon's Lukka warriors	Medium Foot	Protected	Average	Undrilled	-	Impact Foot, Swordsmen	7	6-8	0-8
Thracians	Medium Foot	Protected	Average	Undrilled	-	Light Spear	5	6-8	0-12

SEA PEOPLES

The origin of the Sea Peoples, who played such a major role in the upheavals of the late 13th and early 12th centuries BC is unknown. Numerous theories have been advanced, none of which can be substantiated. Whatever their origin, their sea-borne raids caused increasing pressure on the civilisations of the eastern Mediterranean, several of which collapsed or declined sharply at around this time, as discussed in the notes for their lists.

The Sea Peoples included the Sherden, Peleset, Tjekker, Shekelesh, Denyen, Weshwesh, Lukka, Teresh and Ekwesh. Of these, Peleset, Sherden and Tjekker are all recorded as settled in Philistia (Palestine) by 1100 BC.

This list covers Sea Peoples armies prior to the development of a distinctive Philistine military system around the end of the 12th century BC.

Peleset
Commander

TROOP NOTES

Several of the Sea Peoples are depicted as captives in Egyptian reliefs. The common item of clothing was a tasselled kilt, possibly reinforced with leather strips. In addition to this, Sherden, Peleset, and probably Tjekker and Denyen, wore a leather or bronze cuirass, while Sheklesh and Teresh wore banded leather or linen armour. Sherden wore horned helmets and were armed with a long sword, javelins and a round shield. Peleset, Tjekker and Denyen wore a "tall crown" composed of a circle of upstanding horsehair, reeds, linen or leather strips attached to a decorated head band and fastened by a chin strap. Shields could be studded with possibly bronze bosses.

Some Egyptian-style chariots are depicted, though with three crew (driver and two javelinmen).

Sea Peoples are depicted as carrying their families and belongings in large two-wheeled ox-drawn carts. These would look good as part of a supply camp diorama.

Sherden
Swordsman

SEA PEOPLES STARTER ARMY		
Commander-in-Chief	1	Field Commander
Sub-commander	2	2 x Troop Commander
Chariots	1 BG	4 bases of chariots: Superior, Undrilled Light Chariots – Light Spear
Retinue swordsmen	2 BGs	Each comprising 6 bases of retinue swordsmen: Superior, Armoured, Undrilled Medium Foot – Impact Foot, Swordsmen
Ordinary swordsmen	4 BGs	Each comprising 8 bases of ordinary swordsmen: Average, Protected, Undrilled Medium Foot – Impact Foot, Swordsmen
Javelinmen	2 BGs	Each comprising 6 bases of javelinmen: Average, Unprotected, Undrilled Light Foot – Javelins, Light Spear
Camp	1	Unfortified camp
Total	9 BGs	Camp, 4 mounted bases, 56 foot bases, 3 commanders

BUILDING A CUSTOMISED LIST USING OUR ARMY POINTS

Choose an army based on the maxima and minima in the list below. The following special instructions apply to this army:

- Commanders should be depicted in chariots or as retinue swordsmen.

Peleset Jaelinman

SEA PEOPLES

Territory Types: Agricultural

Troop name	Troop Type				Capabilities		Points per base	Bases per BG	Total bases
C-in-C	Inspired Commander/Field Commander/Troop Commander						80/50/35		1
Sub-commanders	Field Commander						50		0-2
	Troop Commander						35		0-3
	Type	Armour	Quality	Training	Shooting	Close Combat			
Core Troops									
Chariots	Light Chariots	-	Superior	Undrilled	-	Light Spear	15	4-6	0-8
	Heavy Chariots	-	Superior	Undrilled	-	Light Spear	18	4-6	
Retine swordsmen	Medium Foot	Protected	Superior	Undrilled	-	Impact Foot, Swordsmen	9	6-8	0-18
		Armoured					12		
Ordinary swordsmen	Medium Foot	Protected	Average	Undrilled	-	Impact Foot, Swordsmen	7	8-12	32-96
Javelinmen	Light Foot	Unprotected	Average	Undrilled	Javelins	Light Spear	4	6-8	0-24
Optional Troops									
Families	Mob	Unprotected	Poor	Undrilled	-	-	2	8-12	0-12
Fortified camp							24		0-1
Allies									
Libyan allies – Early Libyan									

SEA PEOPLES ALLIES

Troop name	Troop Type				Capabilities		Points per base	Bases per BG	Total bases
Allied commander	Field Commander/Troop Commander						40/25		1
	Type	Armour	Quality	Training	Shooting	Close Combat			
Chariots	Light Chariots	-	Superior	Undrilled	-	Light Spear	15	4	0-4
	Heavy Chariots	-	Superior	Undrilled	-	Light Spear	18	4	
Retine swordsmen	Medium Foot	Protected	Superior	Undrilled	-	Impact Foot, Swordsmen	9	4-6	0-6
		Armoured					12		
Ordinary swordsmen	Medium Foot	Protected	Average	Undrilled	-	Impact Foot, Swordsmen	7	8-12	8-32
Javelinmen	Light Foot	Unprotected	Average	Undrilled	Javelins	Light Spear	4	6-8	0-8

The invasion of the Sea Peoples, by Angus McBride. Taken from Elite 40: New Kingdom Egypt.

PHILISTINE

Descended from Sea Peoples defeated by Egypt in the second quarter of the 12th century BC, the Philistines either carved out their own territory in modern Palestine, or were settled there by Egypt as military colonists but soon asserted their independence. Their name, as well as that of Palestine, derives from the Peleset, one of the Sea People groups. The five principal Philistine cities were Gaza, Ashdod, Ekron, Gath, and Ashkelon. This list covers Philistine armies from their development of a distinct military system c.1100 BC. They lost their independence to Tiglath-Pileser III of Assyria by 732 BC, though there were several revolts thereafter. They eventually became part of the Neo-Babylonian Empire.

Philistine Spearman

PHILISTINE STARTER ARMY

Commander-in-Chief	1	Field Commander
Sub-commander	2	2 x Troop Commander
Chariots	2 BGs	Each comprising 4 bases of chariots: Superior, Drilled Light Chariots – Bow
Elite spearmen	1 BG	6 bases of elite spearmen: Superior, Armoured, Drilled Heavy Foot – Offensive Spearmen
Other spearmen	3 BGs	Each comprising 8 bases of other spearmen: Average, Protected, Undrilled Medium Foot – Offensive Spearmen
Javelinmen	1 BG	6 bases of javelinmen: Average, Unprotected, Undrilled Light Foot – Javelins, Light Spear
Archers	1 BG	8 bases of archers: Average, Unprotected, Undrilled Light Foot – Bow
Slingers	1 BG	6 bases of slingers: Average, Unprotected, Undrilled Light Foot – Sling
Camp	1	Unfortified camp
Total	9 BGs	Camp, 8 mounted bases, 50 foot bases, 3 commanders

BUILDING A CUSTOMISED LIST USING OUR ARMY POINTS

Choose an army based on the maxima and minima in the list below. The following special instructions apply to this army:

- Commanders should be depicted in chariots or as elite spearmen.
- Aramaean allies cannot be used with Kushite Egyptian allies.

Sherden (left), Philistine (right) and Nubian archer (centre), by *Angus McBride*.
Taken from Men-at-Arms 109: *Ancient Armies of the Middle East.*

PHILISTINE

Territory Types: Agricultural, Developed

C-in-C	Inspired Commander/Field Commander/Troop Commander					80/50/35	1	
Sub-commanders	Field Commander					50	0-2	
	Troop Commander					35	0-3	

Troop name		Troop Type				Capabilities		Points per base	Bases per BG	Total bases
		Type	Armour	Quality	Training	Shooting	Close Combat			
Core Troops										
Chariots	Before 800	Light Chariots	-	Superior	Drilled	Bow	-	18	4-6	4-20
	From 800	Heavy Chariots	-	Superior	Drilled	Bow	-	22	4-6	
Elite spearmen		Heavy Foot	Armoured	Superior	Drilled		Offensive Spearmen	13	6-8	0-8
			Protected					10		
Other spearmen		Medium Foot	Protected	Average	Undrilled	-	Offensive Spearmen	7	6-8	16-48
Javelinmen		Light Foot	Unprotected	Average	Undrilled	Javelins	Light Spear	4	6-8	6-32
		Medium Foot	Unprotected	Average	Undrilled	-	Light Spear	4	6-8	
		Medium Foot	Protected	Average	Undrilled	-	Light Spear	5	6-8	0-12
Optional Troops										
Archers		Light Foot	Unprotected	Average	Undrilled	Bow	-	5	6-8	0-12 / 0-12
		Medium Foot	Unprotected	Average	Undrilled	Bow	-	5	4-6	0-6
Slingers		Light Foot	Unprotected	Average	Undrilled	Sling	-	4	6-8	0-8
Hebrew mercenaries		Medium Foot	Armoured	Superior	Drilled	-	Light Spear, Swordsmen	12	4-6	0-6
			Protected	Superior				9		
			Protected	Average				7		
Cavalry	Only from 800	Cavalry	Protected	Average	Drilled	-	Light Spear, Swordsmen	10	4	0-4
Allies										
Aramaean allies – Neo-Hittite and Later Aramaean										
Egyptian allies (Only from 800) – Libyan Egyptian or Kushite Egyptian										
Phoenician allies										

PHILISTINE ALLIES

Allied commander		Field Commander/Troop Commander						40/25	1	
Troop name		Troop Type				Capabilities		Points per base	Bases per BG	Total bases
		Type	Armour	Quality	Training	Shooting	Close Combat			
Chariots	Before 800	Light Chariots	-	Superior	Drilled	Bow	-	18	4-6	4-6
	From 800	Heavy Chariots	-	Superior	Drilled	Bow	-	22	4-6	
Spearmen		Medium Foot	Protected	Average	Undrilled	-	Offensive Spearmen	7	6-8	6-16
Javelinmen		Light Foot	Unprotected	Average	Undrilled	Javelins	Light Spear	4	6-8	0-12
		Medium Foot	Unprotected	Average	Undrilled	-	Light Spear	4	6-8	

PHOENICIAN ALLIES

This list covers allied contingents supplied by the Phoenician cities. Phoenicia was the coastal region of northern Canaan, in modern Lebanon, Syria and Israel. The Phoenicians were great sailors and traders, trading as far away as the British Isles, and planting many colonies in Cyprus and the western Mediterranean. Phoenicia was divided into a number of city-states, of which Tyre and Sidon were the greatest. Phoenicia was ultimately incorporated into the Achaemenid Persian Empire in 539 BC, subsequently providing much of the Persian fleet. Possibly boosted by emigration from the homeland following the Persian conquest, Tyre's largest colony in North Africa, Carthage, grew in power until it ruled an empire in the western Mediterranean before ultimately succumbing to Rome. The armies of Carthage are covered in Field of Glory Companion 3: *Immortal Fire*, and Field of Glory Companion 1: *Rise of Rome*.

- Commanders should be depicted in chariots.
- Spearmen must all be classified the same.

PHOENICIAN ALLIES

Allied commander		Field Commander / Troop Commander						40/25		1	
Troop name		Troop Type				Capabilities		Points per base	Bases per BG	Total bases	
		Type	Armour	Quality	Training	Shooting	Close Combat				
Chariots	Before 800	Light Chariots	-	Superior	Drilled	Bow	-	18	4	0-4	
	From 800	Heavy Chariots	-	Superior	Drilled	Bow	-	22	4		
		Heavy Chariots	-	Superior	Drilled	-	Light Spear	20	4		
Spearmen		Medium Foot	Protected	Average	Drilled	Light Spear	Swordsmen	7	6-8	6-16	
		Medium Foot	Protected	Average	Drilled	-	Offensive Spearmen	8	6-8		
Archers		Light Foot	Unprotected	Average	Undrilled	Bow	-	5	4-6	0-6	
Slingers		Light Foot	Unprotected	Average	Undrilled	Sling	-	4	4	0-4	
Javelinmen		Light Foot	Unprotected	Average	Undrilled	Javelins	Light Spear	4	4		

NEO-HITTITE AND ARAMAEAN

Following the collapse of the Hittite Empire, a number of so-called Neo-Hittite (Syro-Hittite) kingdoms arose in southern Anatolia and northern Syria. In the northern group – including Carchemish, Milid, Tabal, Kummuhu, Hilakku, Quwê & Gurgum – Hittite rulers remained in power. In the southern group – including Unqi, Sam'al, Bit-Adini, Bit-Bahiani, Bit Agusi, Napigu, Hatarikka-Luhuti and Hama – Aramaean rulers came to power around 1000 BC. Aleppo and Damascus were major cities under Aramaean control.

Hadadezer of Damascus and King Ahab of Israel, together with other Aramaean and Neo-

Hittite allies, fought the army of the Assyrian King Shalmaneser III at Qarqar in 853. Though Shalmaneser claims to have won, his advance was halted for the time being.

Neo-Hittite Chariot

Nevertheless the Neo-Hittite and Aramaean kingdoms were gradually conquered by the expanding Assyrian Empire. Carchemish and Milid survived until conquered by Sargon II of Assyria in the late 8th century BC.

This list covers the Neo-Hittite and Aramaean kingdoms of southern Anatolia and Syria from 1100 to 700 BC.

TROOP NOTES

During the 9th and 8th centuries BC Neo-Hittite chariots changed from 2 crew to 4 crew. The number of horses probably changed from 2 to 4 at the same time.

NEO-HITTITE STARTER ARMY		
Commander-in-Chief	1	Field Commander
Sub-commander	2	2 x Troop Commander
Heavy chariots	1 BG	4 bases of heavy chariots: Superior, Drilled Heavy Chariots – Bow
Light chariots	2 BGs	Each comprising 4 bases of light chariots: Superior, Drilled Light Chariots – Bow
Guard spearmen	1 BG	6 bases of guard spearmen: Superior, Protected, Drilled Heavy Foot – Light Spear, Swordsmen
Other regular spearmen	1 BG	8 bases of other regular spearmen: Average, Protected, Drilled Medium Foot – Light Spear, Swordsmen
Aramaean spearmen	2 BGs	Each comprising 6 bases of Aramaean spearmen: Average, Protected, Undrilled Medium Foot – Light Spear
Archers	1 BG	6 bases of archers: Average, Unprotected, Undrilled Light Foot – Bow
Slingers	2 BGs	Each comprising 6 bases of slingers: Average, Unprotected, Undrilled Light Foot – Sling
Camp	1	Unfortified camp
Total	10 BGs	Camp, 12 mounted bases, 44 foot bases, 3 commanders

BUILDING A CUSTOMISED LIST USING OUR ARMY POINTS

Choose an army based on the maxima and minima in the list below. The following special instructions apply to this army:

- Commanders should be depicted in chariots.
- A Neo-Hittite or Aramaean allied commander's contingent must conform to the Neo-Hittite or Aramaean allies list below, but the troops in the contingent are deducted from the minima and maxima in the main list.
- The main army (excluding allied contingents) cannot include more than 16 chariot bases (excluding commanders).

Guard Spearman

NEO-HITTITE AND ARAMAEAN

Territory Types: Agricultural, Developed, Hilly

C-in-C	Inspired Commander/Field Commander/Troop Commander			80/50/35		1	
Sub-commanders	Field Commander/Troop Commander			50/35		0-2	
Neo-Hittite or Aramaean allied commanders	Field Commander/Troop Commander			40/25		0-2	

Troop name	Troop Type				Capabilities		Points per base	Bases per BG	Total bases
	Type	Armour	Quality	Training	Shooting	Close Combat			
Core Troops									
Chariots	Any date	Light Chariots	-	Superior	Drilled	Bow	-	18	4-6	0-24 / 8-24
	Only from 890	Heavy Chariots	-	Superior	Drilled	Bow	-	22	4-6	4-16
Guard spearmen		Heavy Foot	Protected	Superior	Drilled	-	Light Spear, Swordsmen	9	4-6	0-6
Other regular spearmen		Medium Foot	Protected	Average	Drilled	-	Light spear, Swordsmen	7	6-8	0-12
Aramaean spearmen		Medium Foot	Protected	Average	Undrilled	-	Light Spear	5	6-8	12-72
Archers		Light Foot	Unprotected	Average	Undrilled	Bow	-	5	6-8	6-24
		Medium Foot	Unprotected	Average	Undrilled	Bow	-	5	6-8	
Slingers		Light Foot	Unprotected	Average	Undrilled	Sling	-	4	6-8	0-24
Optional Troops									
Camelry		Camelry	Unprotected	Average	Undrilled	Bow	-	10	4	0-4
Cavalry	Only from 890	Cavalry	Protected	Average	Drilled	-	Light Spear, Swordsmen	10	1/2	4-6 / 0-6
		Cavalry	Protected	Average	Drilled	Bow	Swordsmen	12	1/2	
Allies									

Israelite allies (Only from 890) – Later Hebrew

Phoenician allies (Only from 890)

NEO-HITTITE OR ARAMAEAN ALLIES

Allied commander	Field Commander/Troop Commander			40/25		1	

Troop name	Troop Type				Capabilities		Points per base	Bases per BG	Total bases
	Type	Armour	Quality	Training	Shooting	Close Combat			
Chariots	Any date	Light Chariots	-	Superior	Drilled	Bow	-	18	4-6	4-8
	Only from 890	Heavy Chariots	-	Superior	Drilled	Bow	-	22	4-6	
Regular spearmen		Medium Foot	Protected	Average	Drilled	-	Light spear, Swordsmen	7	4-6	0-6
Aramaean spearmen		Medium Foot	Protected	Average	Undrilled	-	Light Spear	5	6-8	0-18
Archers		Light Foot	Unprotected	Average	Undrilled	Bow	-	5	6-8	0-8
		Medium Foot	Unprotected	Average	Undrilled	Bow	-	5	6-8	
Slingers		Light Foot	Unprotected	Average	Undrilled	Sling	-	4	6-8	0-8

LATER HEBREW

The early chronology of the Hebrew kingdoms is fraught, with the very existence of the United Kingdom in dispute. According to the conventional view, King David took the throne in 1000 BC. Circa 920 the United Kingdom split into Israel in the north and Judah in the south. Israel, with its capital Samaria, fell to the Assyrians c.722. Judah persisted until the fall of Jerusalem to the Babylonians in 586.

This list covers Hebrew armies from 1000 to 586 BC.

Hebrew Musician

LATER HEBREW STARTER ARMY		
Commander-in-Chief	1	Field Commander
Sub-commander	2	2 x Troop Commander
Chariots	2 BGs	Each comprising 4 bases of light chariots: Superior, Drilled Light Chariots – Bow
Gibborim	1 BG	8 bases of gibborim: Superior, Armoured, Drilled Medium Foot – Light Spear, Swordsmen
Other spearmen	3 BGs	Each comprising 6 bases of other spearmen: Average, Protected, Undrilled Medium Foot – Light Spear, Swordsmen
Philistine mercenaries	1 BG	8 bases of Philistine mercenaries: Average, Protected, Drilled Medium Foot – Offensive Spearmen
Archers	1 BG	8 bases of archers: Average, Unprotected, Undrilled Light Foot – Bow
Slingers	1 BG	6 bases of slingers: Average, Unprotected, Undrilled Light Foot – Sling
Camp	1	Unfortified camp
Total	9 BGs	Camp, 8 mounted bases, 48 foot bases, 3 commanders

BUILDING A CUSTOMISED LIST USING OUR ARMY POINTS

Choose an army based on the maxima and minima in the list below. The following special instructions apply to this army:

- Commanders should be depicted in chariots or as gibborim.

- Aramaean or Hebrew allies cannot be used with Egyptian, Philistine or Phoenician allies.
- Philistine allies cannot be used with Late Dynastic Egyptian allies.
- Phoenician allies cannot be used with Libyan Egyptian allies.

LATER HEBREW

LATER HEBREW

Territory Types: Agricultural, Developed, Hilly

C-in-C	Inspired Commander/Field Commander/Troop Commander					80/50/35	1	
Sub-commanders	Field Commander					50	0-2	
	Troop Commander					35	0-3	

Troop name		Troop Type				Capabilities		Points per base	Bases per BG	Total bases
		Type	Armour	Quality	Training	Shooting	Close Combat			
Core Troops										
Chariots	Before 800	Light Chariots	-	Superior	Drilled	Bow	-	18	4-6	0-20
	From 800	Heavy Chariots	-	Superior	Drilled	Bow	-	22	4-6	
Gibborim		Medium Foot	Armoured	Superior	Drilled	-	Light Spear, Swordsmen	12	6-8	0-8
			Protected					9		
Other spearmen		Medium Foot	Protected	Average	Undrilled	-	Light spear, Swordsmen	6	6-8	16-72
		Medium Foot	Protected	Average	Undrilled	-	Light spear	5	6-8	
Archers		Light Foot	Unprotected	Average	Undrilled	Bow	-	5	6-8	6-24
Slingers		Light Foot	Unprotected	Average	Undrilled	Sling	-	4	6-8	6-16
Optional Troops										
Philistine or Aegean mercenaries		Medium Foot	Protected	Average	Drilled	-	Offensive Spearmen	8	6-8	0-8
Arab camelry		Camelry	Unprotected	Average	Undrilled	Bow	-	10	4	0-4
Cavalry	Only from 800	Cavalry	Protected	Average	Drilled	-	Light Spear, Swordsmen	10	4	0-4
Allies										
Aramaean allies – Neo-Hittite and Aramaean										
Egyptian allies (Only from 800) – Libyan Egyptian, Kushite Egyptian or Late Dynastic Egyptian – See Field of Glory Companion 3: Immortal Fire										
Hebrew allies – Later Hebrew (Only before 721)										
Philistine allies (Only from 800)										
Phoenician allies (Only from 800)										

LATER HEBREW ALLIES

Allied commander		Field Commander/Troop Commander						40/25	1	
Troop name		Troop Type				Capabilities		Points per base	Bases per BG	Total bases
		Type	Armour	Quality	Training	Shooting	Close Combat			
Chariots	Before 800	Light Chariots	-	Superior	Drilled	Bow	-	18	4-6	0-6
	From 800	Heavy Chariots	-	Superior	Drilled	Bow	-	22	4-6	
Other spearmen		Medium Foot	Protected	Average	Undrilled	-	Light spear, Swordsmen	6	6-8	6-24
		Medium Foot	Protected	Average	Undrilled	-	Light spear	5	6-8	
Archers		Light Foot	Unprotected	Average	Undrilled	Bow	-	5	6-8	0-8
Slingers		Light Foot	Unprotected	Average	Undrilled	Sling	-	4	4-6	0-6

MANNAEAN ALLIES

The Mannaeans lived in the highland regions east of Assyria. This list is based on depictions from the 10th and 9th centuries BC.

- The commander should be depicted as cavalry, or with a bow in a chariot.

MANNAEAN ALLIES									
Allied commander	Field Commander/Troop Commander						40/25		1
Troop name	Troop Type				Capabilities		Points per base	Bases per BG	Total bases
	Type	Armour	Quality	Training	Shooting	Close Combat			
Cavalry	Cavalry	Unprotected	Average	Undrilled	-	Light Spear	6	4	0-4
		Protected					7		
Spearmen	Medium Foot	Protected	Average	Undrilled	-	Light Spear	5	6-8	6-24
Archers	Light Foot	Unprotected	Average	Undrilled	Bow	-	5	6-8	6-16

LIBYAN EGYPTIAN

Following the defeat of the Libyans and Sea Peoples by Ramesses III in the early 12th century BC, large numbers of Libyans were recruited into the army and located in military settlements. They developed into a military caste, named after the tribe of the Meshwesh.

Circa 943 BC the Meshwesh Libyan Shoshenq I seized the throne. He had been commander-in-chief under his predecessor Psusennes II, the last pharaoh of the 21st dynasty. Thus began the 22nd dynasty. Shoshenq campaigned in the Levant, notably against Israel and Judah in 925.

Late in the reign of Orsokon II (874–834), Takelot II, the Libyan High Priest of Amun in Thebes, set himself up as pharaoh. His successors ruled Upper (southern) and Middle Egypt as the 23rd dynasty. The 22nd dynasty thereafter only held sway in Lower (northern) Egypt, ruling from Tanis in the Eastern Delta.

Circa 732 the Prince of Sais in the Western Delta, Tefnakht, set himself up as a rival pharaoh in Lower Egypt, founding the short-lived 24th

dynasty. Expanding his influence southwards, he soon came into conflict with the King of Kush (Nubia) Piye, who had been expanding his influence northwards. Adopting the role of Holy Crusader on behalf of the god Amun, Piye, as first pharaoh of the 25th dynasty, marched north with his army and defeated the northerners at Herakleopolis. The northern kings were forced to submit, though Tefnakht hid on an island in the Delta and submitted only by letter. When Piye returned to Nubia, Tefnakht was once again free to act as he saw fit. Piye's brother and successor, Shabaka, however, extended Kushite control over the whole of Egypt c.720, capturing Sais and burning Tefnakht's successor Bakenrenef alive.

This list covers the armies of the 22nd, 23rd and 24th dynasties of Egypt from 945 to 720 BC.

Royal Guardsman

LIBYAN EGYPTIAN

LIBYAN EGYPTIAN STARTER ARMY

Commander-in-Chief	1	Field Commander
Sub-commander	2	2 x Troop Commander
Chariots	3 BGs	Each comprising 4 bases of chariots: Superior, Drilled Light Chariots – Bow
Royal Guard	1 BG	4 bases of Royal Guard: Superior, Armoured, Drilled Heavy Foot – Impact Foot, Swordsmen
"Invincible Meshwesh"	2 BGs	Each comprising 8 bases of Meshwesh: Superior, Protected, Undrilled Medium Foot – Impact Foot, Swordsmen
Libu javelinmen	2 BGs	Each comprising 8 bases of Libu javelinmen: Average, Unprotected, Drilled Light Foot – Javelins, Light Spear
Camp	1	Unfortified camp
Total	8 BGs	Camp, 12 mounted bases, 36 foot bases, 3 commanders

BUILDING A CUSTOMISED LIST USING OUR ARMY POINTS

Choose an army based on the maxima and minima in the list below. The following special instructions apply to this army:

- Commanders should be depicted in chariots.

- Egyptian close fighters can interpenetrate Egyptian archers and vice versa.

Libu Javelinman

LIBYAN EGYPTIAN

Territory Types: Developed, Agricultural

C-in-C	Inspired Commander/Field Commander/Troop Commander						80/50/35		1	
Sub-commanders	Field Commander						50		0-2	
	Troop Commander						35		0-3	

Troop name	Troop Type				Capabilities		Points per base	Bases per BG	Total bases
	Type	Armour	Quality	Training	Shooting	Close Combat			
Core Troops									
Chariots	Light Chariots	–	Superior	Drilled	Bow	–	18	4-6	6-20
"Invincible Meshwesh"	Medium Foot	Protected	Superior	Undrilled	–	Impact Foot, Swordsmen	9	8-12	8-36
			Average				7		
Libu or other javelinmen	Light Foot	Unprotected	Average	Undrilled	Javelins	Light Spear	4	6-8	12-32
	Medium Foot	Unprotected	Average	Undrilled	–	Light spear	4	6-8	
Optional Troops									
Cavalry	Cavalry	Unprotected	Average	Drilled	–	Light Spear	7	4-6	0-6
				Undrilled			6		
Royal guardsmen	Heavy Foot	Protected	Superior	Drilled	–	Impact Foot, Swordsmen	10	4-6	0-6
		Armoured	Superior				13		
Libu swordsmen	Medium Foot	Unprotected	Average	Undrilled	–	Impact Foot, Swordsmen	6	8-12	0-24
Egyptian close fighters	Medium Foot	Protected	Poor	Drilled	–	Light Spear, Swordsmen	5	6-8	0-18
Egyptian archers	Medium Foot	Unprotected	Poor	Drilled	Bow	–	4	6-8	0-18
Libyan archers	Light Foot	Unprotected	Average	Undrilled	Bow	–	5	6-8	0-8
Nubian archers	Light Foot	Unprotected	Superior	Undrilled	Bow	–	6	6-8	
			Average				5		

LIBYAN EGYPTIAN ALLIES								
Allied commander	Field Commander/Troop Commander					40/25	1	
Troop name	Troop Type				Capabilities		Points per base	Bases per BG	Total bases
	Type	Armour	Quality	Training	Shooting	Close Combat			
Chariots	Light Chariots	-	Superior	Drilled	Bow	-	18	4-6	4-8
"Invincible Meshwesh"	Medium Foot	Protected	Superior	Undrilled	-	Impact Foot, Swordsmen	9	6-12	6-12
			Average				7		
Libu or other javelinmen	Light Foot	Unprotected	Average	Undrilled	Javelins	Light Spear	4	6-8	6-12
	Medium Foot	Unprotected	Average	Undrilled	-	Light spear	4	6-8	

URARTIAN

The Kingdom of Urartu was formed from the unification of a number of small Nairi states by King Aram c.860 BC. It expanded under Sarduri I (834–828), Ishpuini (828–810), Menuas (810–785), Argishti I (785–753) and Sarduri II (753–735) despite frequent attacks by Assyria. At its greatest extent, under Sarduri II, its area corresponded to modern Armenia, south-east Turkey and north-west Iran.

In 714 Rusa I (735–714) suffered a heavy defeat at the hands of invading Cimmerians, most of his generals being killed in the battle.

Despite this, he was able to persuade their main horde to divert away from Urartu, although smaller numbers were allowed to settle in Urartu and subsequently used as mercenaries. Later the same year Rusa's depleted forces suffered a further defeat at the hands of Sargon II of Assyria, the latter going on to sack the main temple at Musasir. Rusa either died of his wounds or committed suicide.

His son Argishti II (714–685), however, was able to maintain peaceful relations with Assyria and restore Urartu's power despite a further defeat

Urartian Royal Army Cavalry

URARTIAN STARTER ARMY

Commander-in-Chief	1	Field Commander
Sub-commander	2	2 x Troop Commander
Chariots	1 BG	4 bases of chariots: Superior, Drilled Heavy Chariots – Bow
Royal army cavalry	1 BG	4 bases of cavalry: Superior, Armoured, Drilled Cavalry – 2 Light Spear, Swordsmen and 2 Bow, Swordsmen
Provincial cavalry	1 BG	4 bases of cavalry: Superior, Armoured, Undrilled Cavalry – 2 Light Spear, Swordsmen and 2 Bow, Swordsmen
Cimmerian mercenaries	1 BG	4 bases of Cimmerian mercenaries: Average, Unprotected, Undrilled Light Horse – Bow, Swordsmen
Guard spearmen	1 BG	6 bases of guard spearmen: Superior, Armoured, Drilled Medium Foot – Light Spear, Swordsmen
Royal army spearmen and archers	1 BG	3 bases of royal army spearmen: Average, Protected, Drilled Medium Foot – Light Spear, Swordsmen, and 3 bases of royal army archers: Average, Protected, Drilled Medium Foot – Bow
Provincial spearmen and archers	2 BGs	Each comprising 4 bases of provincial spearmen: Average, Protected, Undrilled Medium Foot – Light Spear, Swordsmen, and 4 bases of provincial archers: Average, Protected, Undrilled Medium Foot – Bow
Camp	1	Unfortified camp
Total	8 BGs	Camp, 16 mounted bases, 28 foot bases, 3 commanders

by the Cimmerians in 708. An era of relative peace and prosperity continued through the reign of Rusa II (685–645), who made allies of the Cimmerians. However, by the reign of Sardur III (645–635) Urartu had become an Assyrian vassal.

The end of Urartu is shrouded in some mystery. During or soon after the reign of Sardur III, Urartu was invaded by the Skythians and Medes. Many Urartian cities show evidence of destruction by fire around that time. One theory is that the Medes replaced the Aramid dynasty with the later Armenian Orontid dynasty, and that Urartu as their vassal then assisted them in destroying Assyria. Urartu was finally annexed by the Median King Astyages c.585.

This list covers the armies of Urartu from c.860 to c.585 BC.

TROOP NOTES

Urartian foot are depicted with foot spearmen and archers paired together in Assyrian style. The spearmen are shown with shields. Urartu was a centre of metal-working, and Sargon II recorded the capture of 350,000 swords from the sack of Musasir, so we assume that swordsmen capability is justified for the spearmen.

BUILDING A CUSTOMISED LIST USING OUR ARMY POINTS

Choose an army based on the maxima and minima in the list below. The following special instructions apply to this army:

- Commanders should be depicted in chariots.
- The minimum marked * only applies if guard spearmen are used.

URARTIAN

Territory Types: Hilly, Mountains

C-in-C		Inspired Commander/Field Commander/Troop Commander						80/50/35		1	
Sub-commanders		Field Commander						50		0-2	
		Troop Commander						35		0-3	
Troop name		**Troop Type**				**Capabilities**		**Points per base**	**Bases per BG**	**Total bases**	
		Type	Armour	Quality	Training	Shooting	Close Combat				
Core Troops											
Chariots	Any date	Light Chariots	-	Superior	Drilled	Bow	-	18	4-6	0-8	0-8
	Only from 780	Heavy Chariots	-	Superior	Drilled	Bow	-	22	4	0-4	
Cavalry	Only before 750	Cavalry	Protected	Average	Undrilled	-	Light Spear, Swordsmen	9	1/2	4-6	4-12
		Cavalry	Protected	Average	Undrilled	Bow	Swordsmen	11	1/2		
		Cavalry	Protected	Average	Undrilled	Bow*	Light Spear, Swordsmen	11	4-6		
		Cavalry	Protected	Average	Drilled	-	Light Spear, Swordsmen	10	1/2	4-6	
		Cavalry	Protected	Average	Drilled	Bow	Swordsmen	12	1/2		
		Cavalry	Protected	Average	Drilled	Bow*	Light Spear, Swordsmen	12	4-6		
	Only from 750	Cavalry	Armoured	Superior	Undrilled	-	Light Spear, Swordsmen	16	1/2	4-6	8-24
		Cavalry	Armoured	Superior	Undrilled	Bow	Swordsmen	18	1/2		
		Cavalry	Armoured	Superior	Undrilled	Bow*	Light Spear, Swordsmen	18	4-6		
		Cavalry	Armoured	Superior	Drilled	-	Light Spear, Swordsmen	17	1/2	4-6	
		Cavalry	Armoured	Superior	Drilled	Bow	Swordsmen	19	1/2		
		Cavalry	Armoured	Superior	Drilled	Bow*	Light Spear, Swordsmen	19	4-6		
Royal Army spearmen and supporting archers		Medium Foot	Protected	Average	Drilled	-	Light Spear, Swordsmen	7	1/2	6-8	*6-36
		Medium Foot	Protected	Average	Drilled	Bow	-	7	1/2		
Provincial spearmen and supporting archers		Medium Foot	Protected	Average	Undrilled	-	Light Spear, Swordsmen	6	1/2 or all	6-8	12-78
		Medium Foot	Protected	Average	Undrilled	Bow	-	6	1/2 or 0		
Optional Troops											
Scouts		Light Horse	Unprotected	Average	Undrilled	Bow	-	8	4	0-4	
Cimmerian mercenaries	Only from 714	Light Horse or Cavalry	Unprotected	Average	Undrilled	Bow	Swordsmen	10	4	0-4	
Guard spearmen	Only from 750	Medium or Heavy Foot	Armoured	Superior	Drilled	-	Light Spear, Swordsmen	12	4-6	0-6	
Separately deployed archers		Light Foot	Unprotected	Average	Undrilled	Bow	-	5	6-8	0-24	
Levy dregs		Mob	Unprotected	Poor	Undrilled	-	-	2	8-12	0-12	
Fortified camp								24		0-1	
Allies											
Cimmerian or Skythian allies (Only from 750) – Cimmerian or Early Skythian											
Median allies (Only from 750)											
Musasirian allies – Mannaean											
Neo-Hittite allies (Only from 780 to 750) – Neo-Hittite and Aramaean											

URARTIAN ALLIES									
Allied commander		Field Commander/Troop Commander					40/25	1	
Troop name	Troop Type				Capabilities		Points per base	Bases per BG	Total bases
	Type	Armour	Quality	Training	Shooting	Close Combat			
Chariots	Light Chariots	-	Superior	Drilled	Bow	-	18	4	0-4
	Heavy Chariots	-	Superior	Drilled	Bow	-	22	4	
Cavalry	Cavalry	Armoured	Superior	Undrilled	-	Light Spear, Swordsmen	16	1/2	4-8
	Cavalry	Armoured	Superior	Undrilled	Bow	Swordsmen	18	1/2	
	Cavalry	Armoured	Superior	Undrilled	Bow*	Light Spear, Swordsmen	18	4-6	
	Cavalry	Armoured	Superior	Drilled	-	Light Spear, Swordsmen	17	1/2	
	Cavalry	Armoured	Superior	Drilled	Bow	Swordsmen	19	1/2	
	Cavalry	Armoured	Superior	Drilled	Bow*	Light Spear, Swordsmen	19	4-6	
Royal Army spearmen and supporting archers	Medium Foot	Protected	Average	Drilled	-	Light Spear, Swordsmen	7	1/2	0-12
	Medium Foot	Protected	Average	Drilled	Bow	-	7	1/2	
Provincial spearmen and supporting archers	Medium Foot	Protected	Average	Undrilled	-	Light Spear, Swordsmen	6	1/2 or all	6-24
	Medium Foot	Protected	Average	Undrilled	Bow	-	6	1/2 or 0	
Separately deployed archers	Light Foot	Unprotected	Average	Undrilled	Bow	-	5	6-8	0-8

MEDIAN

The Iranian Medes first appear in history in 836 BC when they are recorded as paying tribute to the Assyrian king Shalmaneser III. At this stage their lands were situated in the Zagros Mountains in modern northern Iran and they were divided into many separate groups under local chieftains. Despite frequent rebellions, they continued to pay tribute to the Assyrians well into the 7th century BC. For part of that century they may have been under Skythian domination.

Under Cyaxares (Uvaxštra) (625–585) the Medes were united and the Skyths either overthrown or incorporated. In 615 he invaded Assyria and in 612 an alliance of the Medes and Babylonians took the Assyrian capital, Nineveh. The Assyrian Empire rapidly collapsed, with the Babylonians eventually taking over most of its former territory, while the Medes controlled the highland regions to the north and east. Cyaxares then came into conflict with the Kingdom of Lydia in western Anatolia (in modern Turkey). The border was eventually drawn on the River Halys in central Anatolia. By the end of his reign the Median Empire included modern Iran, Armenia, Azerbaijan, northern Iraq and eastern Turkey.

The next king Astyages (Ištovigu) (585–550), however, was overthrown by his daughter's son, the Achaemenid Cyrus (Kūruš) II of Persia, who thus transformed the Median Empire into the Achaemenid Persian Empire.

Median Archer

The Medes continued to enjoy high status in the Persian Empire, which can properly be regarded as a continuation of the Median Empire under a new dynasty.

This list covers Median armies from 836 to 550 BC.

TROOP NOTES

Classification of Median troops is largely speculative – we give a choice of interpretations.

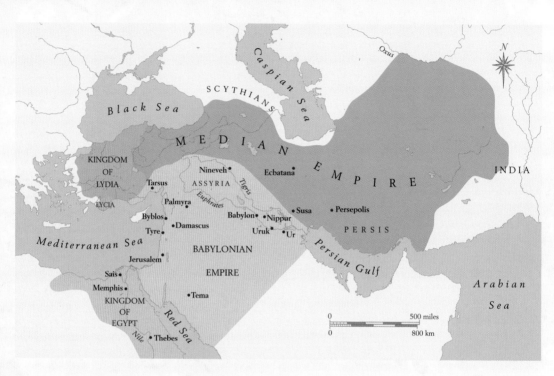

The Median Empire, 550 BC. Taken from Shadows in the Desert: Ancient Persia at War.

MEDIAN STARTER ARMY		
Commander-in-Chief	1	Field Commander
Sub-commander	2	2 x Troop Commander
Median cavalry	3 BGs	Each comprising 4 bases of Median cavalry: Superior, Armoured, Undrilled Cavalry – Bow, Swordsmen
Light horse archers	3 BGs	Each comprising 4 bases of light horse archers: Average, Unprotected, Undrilled Light Horse – Bow, Swordsmen
Median spearmen and archers	3 BGs	Each comprising 8 bases of Median spearmen and archers: Average, Protected, Undrilled Medium Foot – 4 Bow, Light Spear and 4 Bow
Camp	1	Unfortified camp
Total	9 BGs	Camp, 24 mounted bases, 24 foot bases, 3 commanders

BUILDING A CUSTOMISED LIST USING OUR ARMY POINTS

Choose an army based on the maxima and minima in the list below. The following special instructions apply to this army:

- Commanders should be depicted as cavalry.
- Median spearmen battle groups can either be all MF spearmen, 2/3 MF spearmen and 1/3 LF archers or 1/2 MF bow/spearmen and 1/2 MF bowmen. All spearmen battle groups must conform to the same one of these three interpretations.
- The minimum marked * only applies if spearmen are in unmixed spearmen only battle groups.

MEDIAN

Territory Types: Agricultural, Developed, Hilly

C-in-C	Inspired Commander/Field Commander/Troop Commander						80/50/35	1	
Sub-commanders	Field Commander						50	0-2	
	Troop Commander						35	0-3	

Troop name	Troop Type				Capabilities		Points per base	Bases per BG	Total bases
	Type	Armour	Quality	Training	Shooting	Close Combat			
Core Troops									
Median cavalry	Cavalry	Armoured	Superior	Undrilled	Bow	Swordsmen	18	4-6	0-16 / 8-32
	Cavalry	Protected	Superior	Undrilled	Bow	Swordsmen	14	4-6	0-32
			Average				11		
	Cavalry	Unprotected	Average	Undrilled	Bow	Swordsmen	10	4-6	
Median spearmen and archers	Medium Foot	Protected	Average	Undrilled	-	Light Spear	5	2/3 or all / 6-9	16-80
	Light Foot	Unprotected	Average	Undrilled	Bow	-	5	1/3 or 0	
	Medium Foot	Protected	Average	Undrilled	Bow	Light Spear	6	1/2 / 6-8	
	Medium Foot	Protected	Average	Undrilled	Bow	-	6	1/2	
Separately deployed Median archers	Light Foot	Unprotected	Average	Undrilled	Bow	-	5	6-8	*8-32
	Medium Foot	Unprotected	Average	Undrilled	Bow	-	5	6-8	
Optional Troops									
Subject or mercenary light horse archers	Only from 626	Light Horse	Unprotected	Average	Undrilled	Bow	Swordsmen	10	4-6	0-12
		Cavalry	Unprotected	Average	Undrilled	Bow	Swordsmen	10	4-6	
		Light Horse	Unprotected	Average	Undrilled	Bow	-	8	4-6	
Subject spearmen	Only from 626	Medium Foot	Protected	Average / Poor	Undrilled	-	Light Spear	5 / 3	6-8	0-12
Subject foot archers	Only from 626	Light foot	Unprotected	Average / Poor	Undrilled	Bow	-	5 / 3	6-8	0-12
		Medium Foot	Unprotected	Average / Poor	Undrilled	Bow	-	5 / 3	6-8	
		Medium Foot	Unprotected	Average	Undrilled	Bow	Light Spear	5	1/2 / 6-8	
						Bow	-	5	1/2	
		Medium Foot	Unprotected	Poor	Undrilled	Bow	Light Spear	3	1/2 / 6-8	
						Bow	-	3	1/2	
Allies									

Assyrian allies (Only before 668) – Neo-Assyrian Empire

Babylonian allies (Only from 626) – Neo-Babylonian Empire

Cimmerian or Skythian allies – Cimmerian or Early Skythia

MEDIAN ALLIES								
Allied commander		Field Commander/Troop Commander				40/25		1
Troop name	Troop Type				Capabilities		Points per base	Bases per BG	Total bases
	Type	Armour	Quality	Training	Shooting	Close Combat			
Median cavalry	Cavalry	Armoured	Superior	Undrilled	Bow	Swordsmen	18	4-6	0-6	4-12
	Cavalry	Protected	Superior	Undrilled	Bow	Swordsmen	14	4-6	0-12	
			Average				11			
	Cavalry	Unprotected	Average	Undrilled	Bow	Swordsmen	10	4-6		
Median spearmen and archers	Medium Foot	Protected	Average	Undrilled	-	Light Spear	5	2/3 or all	6-9	6-24
	Light Foot	Unprotected	Average	Undrilled	Bow	-	5	1/3 or 0		
	Medium Foot	Protected	Average	Undrilled	Bow	Light Spear	6	1/2	6-8	
	Medium Foot	Protected	Average	Undrilled	Bow	-	6	1/2		
Separately deployed Median archers	Light Foot	Unprotected	Average	Undrilled	Bow	-	5	6-8	0-12	
	Medium Foot	Unprotected	Average	Undrilled	Bow	-	5	6-8		

NEO-ELAMITE

Elam was the region south-east of Mesopotamia, in modern Iran. Its history dates back before 3,000 BC. This list covers Elamite armies from the late 9th century BC until Susa fell to the Achaemenids in 539 BC.

Elam was frequently allied with Babylon against Assyria. Under King Urtaku (676–664) a brief rapprochement with Assyria was followed by further war. Elamite assistance to the rebel Shamash-shum-ukin was rewarded by the Assyrian invasion of Elam and sack of Susa c.646. Following this Elam was fragmented into a number of small kingdoms. By 539 Susa was in the hands of the Achaemenids.

TROOP NOTES

Elamite chariots were pulled by either two or four small horses or mules and carried a driver and up to three archers who sat or knelt on an open platform. Lacking the equipment for close combat, it is questionable whether any of them merit classification as Heavy Chariots. We therefore offer a choice of classification – either 2-horse chariots can be graded as Light Chariots and 4-horse as Heavy, or all can be classified as Light. The lightness of the crews' equipment and rudimentary nature of the chariots compared with those of other nations is also reflected by Average quality rating.

We know from Assyrian sources that some Elamite infantry were equipped with spear, shield and bow, though they are never depicted. To allow for different interpretations we give a choice of classification.

Neo-Elamite Commander

62

NEO-ELAMITE STARTER ARMY

Commander-in-Chief	1	Troop Commander
Sub-commander	2	2 x Troop Commander
Chariots	5 BGs	Each comprising 4 bases of chariots: Average, Undrilled Light Chariots – Bow
Cavalry	1 BG	4 bases of cavalry: Average, Unprotected, Undrilled Cavalry – Bow*, Light Spear, Swordsmen
Archers	4 BGs	Each comprising 6 bases of archers: Average, Unprotected, Undrilled Light Foot – Bow
Shielded spearmen and archers	2 BGs	Each comprising 6 bases of Average, Protected, Undrilled Medium Foot – half Bow, Light Spear, half Bow
Camp	1	Unfortified camp
Total	12 BGs	Camp, 24 mounted bases, 36 foot bases, 3 commanders

BUILDING A CUSTOMISED LIST USING OUR ARMY POINTS

Choose an army based on the maxima and minima in the list below. The following special instructions apply to this army:

- Commanders should be depicted in chariots.

- Shielded spearmen and archers battle groups can either be classified as half light spear, swordsmen, half bow or half bow, light spear, half bow. All such battle groups must be classified the same.

NEO-ELAMITE

Territory Types: Agricultural, Hilly

Troop name	Troop Type				Capabilities		Points per base	Bases per BG	Total bases
C-in-C	Inspired Commander/Field Commander/Troop Commander						80/50/35	1	
Sub-commanders	Field Commander						50	0-2	
	Troop Commander						35	0-3	
	Type	Armour	Quality	Training	Shooting	Close Combat			
Core Troops									
Chariots	Heavy Chariots	-	Average	Undrilled	Bow	-	16	4-6	0-12, 4-28
	Light Chariots	-	Average	Undrilled	Bow	-	13	4-6	0-28
Cavalry	Cavalry	Unprotected	Average	Undrilled	Bow*	Light Spear, Swordsmen	10	4-6	4-12
Archers	Light Foot	Unprotected	Average	Undrilled	Bow	-	5	6-8	24-112
	Medium Foot	Unprotected	Average	Undrilled	Bow	-	5	6-8	
Optional Troops									
Shielded spearmen and archers	Medium Foot	Protected	Average	Undrilled	-	Light Spear, Swordsmen	6	1/2, 6-8	0-16
	Medium Foot	Protected	Average	Undrilled	Bow	-	6	1/2	
	Medium Foot	Protected	Average	Undrilled	Bow	Light Spear	6	1/2, 6-8	
	Medium Foot	Protected	Average	Undrilled	Bow	-	6	1/2	
Allies									
Babylonian allies – Neo-Babylonian Empire									
Arab allies – Proto-Arab									

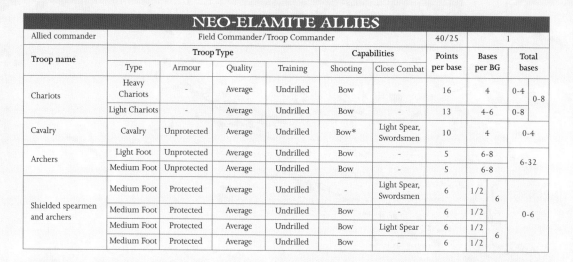

NEO-ELAMITE ALLIES

Allied commander	Field Commander/Troop Commander						40/25		1	
Troop name	**Troop Type**				**Capabilities**		**Points per base**	**Bases per BG**	**Total bases**	
	Type	Armour	Quality	Training	Shooting	Close Combat				
Chariots	Heavy Chariots	-	Average	Undrilled	Bow	-	16	4	0-4	0-8
	Light Chariots	-	Average	Undrilled	Bow	-	13	4-6	0-8	
Cavalry	Cavalry	Unprotected	Average	Undrilled	Bow*	Light Spear, Swordsmen	10	4	0-4	
Archers	Light Foot	Unprotected	Average	Undrilled	Bow	-	5	6-8	6-32	
	Medium Foot	Unprotected	Average	Undrilled	Bow	-	5	6-8		
Shielded spearmen and archers	Medium Foot	Protected	Average	Undrilled	-	Light Spear, Swordsmen	6	1/2	6	0-6
	Medium Foot	Protected	Average	Undrilled	Bow	-	6	1/2		
	Medium Foot	Protected	Average	Undrilled	Bow	Light Spear	6	1/2	6	
	Medium Foot	Protected	Average	Undrilled	Bow	-	6	1/2		

PROTO-ARAB ALLIES

Allied commander	Field Commander/Troop Commander						40/25		1	
Troop name	**Troop Type**				**Capabilities**		**Points per base**	**Bases per BG**	**Total bases**	
	Type	Armour	Quality	Training	Shooting	Close Combat				
Camelry	Camelry	Unprotected	Average	Undrilled	Bow	-	10	4-6	4-12	
Foot warriors	Medium Foot	Protected	Average	Undrilled	-	Light Spear	5	6-8	0-16	
Skirmishers	Light Foot	Unprotected	Average	Undrilled	Javelins	Light Spear	4			
	Light Foot	Unprotected	Average	Undrilled	Bow	-	5	4-6	0-8	
	Light Foot	Unprotected	Average	Undrilled	Sling	-	4			

CIMMERIAN OR EARLY SKYTHIAN

This list covers Cimmerian armies from the mid-8th century BC when they were driven from the steppes by the Skythians, until c.630 BC when they were decisively defeated by Alyattes II of Lydia. In the interim they ravaged Phrygia, Cilicia and Lydia. It also covers Skythian armies prior to 550 BC.

CIMMERIAN STARTER ARMY

Commander-in-Chief	1	Troop Commander
Sub-commander	2	2 x Troop Commander
Best cavalry	3 BGs	Each comprising 4 bases of best cavalry: Superior, Protected, Undrilled Cavalry – Bow, Swordsmen
Other cavalry	8 BGs	Each comprising 4 bases of other cavalry: Average, Unprotected, Undrilled Light Horse – Bow, Swordsmen
Camp	1	Unfortified camp
Total	11 BGs	Camp, 44 mounted bases, 3 commanders

Skythian king and wounded Urartian nobleman, by *Angus McBride.*
Taken from **Men-at-Arms 137: The Scythians 700–300 BC.**

BUILDING A CUSTOMISED LIST USING OUR ARMY POINTS

Choose an army based on the maxima and minima in the list below. The following special instructions apply to this army:

- Commanders should be depicted as cavalry.
- Thracian allies cannot be used with Mannaeans or Urartians.
- The minima marked * apply if any foot are used.

CIMMERIAN OR EARLY SKYTHIAN

	Territory Types: Steppe								
C-in-C	Inspired Commander/Field Commander/Troop Commander						80/50/35		1
Sub-commanders	Field Commander						50		0-2
	Troop Commander						35		0-3
Troop name	Troop Type				Capabilities		Points per base	Bases per BG	Total bases
	Type	Armour	Quality	Training	Shooting	Close Combat			
Core Troops									
Best cavalry	Cavalry	Protected	Superior	Undrilled	Bow	Swordsmen	14	4-6	0-12
Other cavalry	Light Horse or Cavalry	Unprotected	Average	Undrilled	Bow	Swordsmen	10	4-6	16-76
Foot archers	Light Foot	Unprotected	Average	Undrilled	Bow	-	5	6-8	*12-24
			Poor				3		
	Medium Foot	Unprotected	Average	Undrilled	Bow	-	5	6-8	
			Poor				3		
Foot spearmen	Medium Foot	Protected	Average	Undrilled	-	Light Spear	5	6-8	*8-24
			Poor				3		
Allies									
Only Cimmerians									
Mannaean allies									
Thracian allies – See Field of Glory Companion 3: *Immortal Fire*									
Urartian allies									
Only Skythians									
Cimmerian allies – Cimmerian or Early Skythian									

CIMMERIAN OR EARLY SKYTHIAN ALLIES

Allied commander	Field Commander/Troop Commander						40/25		1
Troop name	Troop Type				Capabilities		Points per base	Bases per BG	Total bases
	Type	Armour	Quality	Training	Shooting	Close Combat			
Best cavalry	Cavalry	Protected	Superior	Undrilled	Bow	Swordsmen	14	4	0-4
Other cavalry	Light Horse or Cavalry	Unprotected	Average	Undrilled	Bow	Swordsmen	10	4-6	4-24
Foot archers	Light Foot	Unprotected	Average	Undrilled	Bow	-	5	6-8	0-8
			Poor				3		
	Medium Foot	Unprotected	Average	Undrilled	Bow	-	5	6-8	
			Poor				3		
Foot spearmen	Medium Foot	Protected	Average	Undrilled	-	Light Spear	5	6-8	0-8
			Poor				3		

Skythian horse archers, by Angus McBride. Taken from Elite 120: Mounted Archers of the Steppe 600 BC–AD 1300.

NEO-ASSYRIAN EMPIRE

In 745 BC, a general called Pulu seized the crown of Assyria and took the regnal name Tiglath-Pileser III (745–727). He made sweeping reforms of the government. Henceforth the vassal states were annexed and administered as provinces by formal bureaucracies. A regular standing army (*kisir sharruti*) was formed, backed up by reservists (*sab sharri*) in time of war and a general levy (*dikut-mati*) in emergencies. A large body of royal guard troops (*qurubuti sha shepe*) was also maintained. Standing army troops were stationed throughout the Empire, backed up by locally recruited contingents. A less successful policy, in the long term, was the practice of mass-deportations from conquered territories to other provinces of the Empire. While this presumably reduced the immediate risk of revolts, it cannot have endeared the Assyrians to their subjects.

Assyrian policy was one of relentless expansion. Babylon was conquered in 729, Lower (northern) Egypt in 671. In between these two conquests,

Guard Spearman Battle Group

Assyrian troops in Babylonia, early 7th century BC, by Angus McBride. Taken from Elite 39: The Ancient Assyrians.

most of the remaining independent states in the Levant had been annexed. At its greatest extent, at the end of the reign of Esarhaddon (681–669) the Empire stretched from Mesopotamia (modern Iraq) in the East to Cilicia (in southern Turkey) in the north-west, and Lower Egypt in the south-west. In the north and east, however, the Cimmerians, the Kingdom of Urartu, the Medes and the Kingdom of Elam were a constant threat – often defeated but never conquered.

The cracks started to appear in the reign of Ashurbanipal (669–c.631/627). Ashurbanipal's elder brother, Shamash-shum-ukin, King (governor) of Babylon, revolted in 652 with the aid of the local Chaldaean tribes and the King of Elam. His revolt was not suppressed until 648 when Babylon fell and Shamash-shum-ukin immolated himself in his burning palace. Following this Elam was invaded and its capital Susa leveled. During the war, however, Egypt took the opportunity of seceding under Psamtik I.

Following Ashurbanipal's death the situation rapidly deteriorated. In 626, the Chaldaean Nabopolassar (Nabû-apal-usur), governor of the Sea-Land, rose in revolt and was in control of Babylon by 625. A desultory war ensued. In 615 the Medes, under Cyaxares (Uvaxštra), invaded. The Assyrian religious capital, Ashur, fell to them in 614. An alliance between the Medes and the Babylonians was sealed by the marriage of Cyaxares's grand-daughter to Nabopolassar's son.

The Assyrians sought Egyptian help, but this did not arrive in time to prevent the Assyrian capital, Nineveh, falling to the allies in 612. The last major Assyrian centre, Harran, fell in 610. An attempt to recover it with Egyptian help in 609 failed.

This list covers the armies of Assyria from 745 to 609 BC.

TROOP NOTES

Chariots were almost certainly pulled by four horses. At the start of the period most had three crewmen, though some had four. By the reign of Ashurbanipal, if not earlier, the standard crew was four.

The role of cavalry rapidly gained in importance. Though qurubuti at least were equipped with both bow and spear, it is clear from evidence relating to later periods of history that it was difficult to train troops to be equally adept with both weapons. We therefore classify Assyrian cavalry either as all Bow*/Light Spear, or front rank Light Spear, rear rank Bow. If "other cavalry" battle groups are fielded as Bow*/Light Spear, bowmen without spears are assumed to make up the rear ranks of each base, allowing shallower formations to be represented.

We treat foot spearmen equipped with tower shields or very large round shields as Heavy Foot. Those with smaller round shields are treated as Medium Foot.

Assyrian royal guardsmen, 7th century BC, by Angus McBride. Taken from Elite 39: The Ancient Assyrians.

NEO-ASSYRIAN EMPIRE STARTER ARMY

Commander-in-Chief	1	Field Commander
Sub-commander	2	2 x Troop Commander
Chariots	2 BGs	Each comprising 4 bases of chariots: Superior, Drilled Heavy Chariots – Bow
Cavalry	2 BGs	Each comprising 4 bases of cavalry: Superior, Armoured, Drilled Cavalry – 2 Light Spear, Swordsmen and 2 Bow, Swordsmen
Unarmoured tower shield spearmen and archers	1 BG	4 bases of unarmoured tower shield spearmen: Average, Protected, Drilled Heavy Foot – Light Spear, Swordsmen, and 4 bases of archers: Average, Protected, Drilled Medium Foot – Bow
Unarmoured round shield spearmen and archers	1 BG	4 bases of unarmoured round shield spearmen: Average, Protected, Drilled Medium Foot – Light Spear, Swordsmen, and 4 bases of archers: Average, Protected, Drilled Medium Foot – Bow
Tribal levy archers	1 BG	8 bases of tribal levy archers: Poor, Unprotected, Undrilled Light Foot – Bow
Tribal levy slingers	2 BGs	Each comprising 6 bases of tribal levy slingers: Poor, Unprotected, Undrilled Light Foot – Sling
Camp	1	Unfortified camp
Total	9 BGs	Camp, 16 mounted bases, 36 foot bases, 3 commanders

BUILDING A CUSTOMISED LIST USING OUR ARMY POINTS

Choose an army based on the maxima and minima in the list below. The following special instructions apply to this army:

- Commanders should be depicted in chariots.
- Elamites, Mannaians, Medes, Persians or Phrygians cannot be used with Egyptians, Hebrews or Philistines.

NEO-ASSYRIAN EMPIRE

Territory Types: Agricultural, Developed, Hilly

Troop name		Troop Type				Capabilities		Points per base	Bases per BG	Total bases
C-in-C		Inspired Commander/Field Commander/Troop Commander						80/50/35		1
Sub-commanders		Field Commander						50		0-2
		Troop Commander						35		0-3
		Type	Armour	Quality	Training	Shooting	Close Combat			
Core Troops										
Chariots		Heavy Chariots	-	Superior	Drilled	Bow	-	22	4-6	4-18
Guard cavalry		Cavalry	Armoured	Elite	Drilled	Bow*	Light Spear, Swordsmen	22	4-6	0-6
				Superior				19		
Other cavalry	Only before 704	Cavalry	Protected	Average	Drilled	Bow*	Light Spear, Swordsmen	12	4-6	4-12
		Cavalry	Protected	Average	Drilled	-	Light Spear, Swordsmen	10	1/2 4-6	
		Cavalry	Protected	Average	Drilled	Bow	Swordsmen	12	1/2	
	Only from 704	Cavalry	Armoured	Superior	Drilled	Bow*	Light Spear, Swordsmen	19	4-6	4-18
				Average				15		
		Cavalry	Armoured	Superior	Drilled	-	Light Spear, Swordsmen	17	1/2 4-6	
				Average				13		
		Cavalry	Armoured	Superior	Drilled	Bow	Swordsmen	19	1/2	
				Average				15		

Guard spearmen	Only before 704	Medium Foot	Armoured	Superior	Drilled	-	Light Spear, Swordsmen	12	All or 2/3	4-9	0-9
	Only from 704	Heavy Foot	Armoured	Superior	Drilled	-	Light Spear, Swordsmen	12			
Guard archers		Light Foot	Unprotected	Superior	Drilled	Bow	-	6	0 or 1/3		
Armoured spearmen and archers	Only from 681	Heavy Foot	Armoured	Average	Drilled	-	Light Spear, Swordsmen	9	1/2	6-8	0-8
		Medium Foot	Armoured	Average	Drilled	Bow	-	9	1/2		
Unarmoured spearmen	Any date	Medium Foot	Protected	Average	Drilled	-	Light Spear, Swordsmen	7	1/2	6-8	8-24
	Only from 681	Heavy Foot	Protected	Average	Drilled	-	Light Spear, Swordsmen	7			
Unarmoured archers		Medium Foot	Protected	Average	Drilled	Bow	-	7	1/2		
Tribal levies		Light Foot	Unprotected	Average	Undrilled	Bow	-	5		6-8	0-16
				Poor				3			
		Light Foot	Unprotected	Average	Undrilled	Sling	-	4		6-8	0-16	6-24
				Poor				2			
		Light Foot	Unprotected	Average	Undrilled	Javelins	Light Spear	4		4-6	0-6
				Poor				2			

Optional Troops											
Mounted scouts		Light Horse	Unprotected	Average	Drilled	Bow	-	8	4		0-4
Cimmerian regiment	Only from 679	Light Horse or Cavalry	Unprotected	Average	Undrilled	Bow	Swordsmen	10	4		
Arab levy camelry		Camelry	Unprotected	Poor	Undrilled	Bow	-	8	4		0-4
Egyptian or Kushite regiments		Medium Foot	Unprotected	Average	Drilled	Bow	-	6	4-6		0-6
Reserve foot		Medium Foot	Protected	Poor	Drilled	-	Light Spear, Swordsmen	5	1/2	8-12	0-12
		Medium Foot	Protected	Poor	Drilled	Bow	-	5	1/2		
Other levies		Mob	Unprotected	Poor	Undrilled	-	-	2	8-12		0-12
Field fortifications		Field Fortifications						3			0-8
Fortified camp								24			0-1

Allies
Arab vassals – Proto-Arab
Aramaean and Neo-Hittite allies (Only before 704)
Cimmerian allies (Only before 704) – Cimmerian or Early Skythian
Egyptian vassals or allies (Only before 704 – Libyan Egyptian, or from 681 – Late Dynastic Egyptian – See Field of Glory Companion 3: Immortal Fire
Elamite allies (Only from 668 to 665) – Neo-Elamite
Israelite vassals (Only before 722) – Later Hebrew
Mannaean vassals or allies
Median or Persian vassals or allies – Median
Philistine vassals
Phrygian allies (Only before 681)
Skythian allies (Only from 681) – Cimmerian or Early Skythian

NEO-ASSYRIAN EMPIRE ALLIES

Allied commander				Field Commander/Troop Commander				40/25	1	
Troop name		**Troop Type**				**Capabilities**		**Points per base**	**Bases per BG**	**Total bases**
		Type	Armour	Quality	Training	Shooting	Close Combat			
Chariots		Heavy Chariots	-	Superior	Drilled	Bow	-	22	4-6	4-6
Other cavalry	Only before 704	Cavalry	Protected	Average	Drilled	Bow*	Light Spear, Swordsmen	12	4	0-4
		Cavalry	Protected	Average	Drilled	-	Light Spear, Swordsmen	10	1/2	
		Cavalry	Protected	Average	Drilled	Bow	Swordsmen	12	1/2	4
	Only from 704	Cavalry	Armoured	Superior	Drilled	Bow*	Light Spear, Swordsmen	19	4-6	4-6
				Average				15		
		Cavalry	Armoured	Superior	Drilled	-	Light Spear, Swordsmen	17	1/2	4-6
				Average				13		
		Cavalry	Armoured	Superior	Drilled	Bow	Swordsmen	19	1/2	
				Average				15		
Unarmoured spearmen	Any date	Medium Foot	Protected	Average	Drilled	-	Light Spear, Swordsmen	7	1/2	0-8
	Only from 681	Heavy Foot	Protected	Average	Drilled	-	Light Spear, Swordsmen	7	6-8	0-8
Unarmoured archers		Medium Foot	Protected	Average	Drilled	Bow	-	7	1/2	
Tribal levies		Light Foot	Unprotected	Average	Undrilled	Bow	-	5	6-8	0-8
				Poor				3		
		Light Foot	Unprotected	Average	Undrilled	Sling	-	4	6-8	0-8
				Poor				2		

PHRYGIAN ALLIES

Following the fall of the Hittite Empire, the Phrygians (known to the Assyrians as Mushki) lived in northern and central Anatolia (in modern Turkey). The Phrygian Kingdom was overwhelmed by the Cimmerians c.690 BC and subsequently annexed by Lydia.

• The commander should be depicted as cavalry, or in a chariot.

PHRYGIAN ALLIES

Allied commander				Field Commander/Troop Commander			40/25	1	
Troop name	**Troop Type**				**Capabilities**		**Points per base**	**Bases per BG**	**Total bases**
	Type	Armour	Quality	Training	Shooting	Close Combat			
Chariots	Light Chariots	-	Superior	Undrilled	-	Light Spear	15	4	0-4
Cavalry	Cavalry	Protected	Average	Undrilled	-	Light Spear, Swordsmen	9	4	0-4
		Unprotected					8		
Spearmen	Medium Foot	Protected	Average	Undrilled	-	Light Spear	5	6-8	6-24
Archers	Light Foot	Unprotected	Average	Undrilled	Bow	-	5	4-6	0-6
Javelinmen	Light Foot	Unprotected	Average	Undrilled	Javelins	Light Spear	5	4-6	0-6

KUSHITE EGYPTIAN

Circa 732 BC the King of Kush (Nubia), Piye, invaded Egypt and established the 25th dynasty, ruling from Napata in Nubia. His brother and successor Shabaqa consolidated Kushite control by capturing Sais and burning alive the last pharaoh of the 24th dynasty, Bakenrenef.

In the reign of Taharqa (690–664), King Esarhaddon of Assyria conquered Lower (northern) Egypt, but allowed the local dynasts to retain their small kingdoms as a counterbalance to Kushite power. Following Esarhaddon's death, Taharqa persuaded the Lower Egyptian kinglets to revolt. They were defeated by Esarhaddon's successor Ashurbanipal, however, and deported to Assyria.

Necho I, a grandson of Bakenrenef, was set up by the Assyrians as ruler of Memphis and Sais.

In 664 Taharqa's successor, Tantamani, invaded Lower Egypt and killed Necho. The Assyrians counter-invaded and advanced into Upper (southern) Egypt where they sacked Thebes. In 656 Necho's son and successor Psamtik I took a fleet to Thebes, where he forced the High Priestess of Amun to recognise his daughter as her successor. This marked the re-unification of Egypt and the expulsion of the Kushite dynasty, who nevertheless remained in power in Nubia. Circa 650 Psamtik seceded from Assyria, becoming the first pharaoh of the 26th dynasty. 26th dynasty armies are covered by the Late Dynastic Egyptian list in Field of Glory Army Companion 3: *Immortal Fire*.

This list covers the armies of the Kushite 25th dynasty of Egypt from 732 to 656 BC.

Egyptian Hereditary Archer

KUSHITE EGYPTIAN STARTER ARMY		
Commander-in-Chief	1	Field Commander
Sub-commander	2	2 x Troop Commander
Kushite heavy chariots	2 BGs	Each comprising 4 bases of heavy chariots: Superior, Undrilled Heavy Chariots – Bow
Kushite light chariots	2 BGs	Each comprising 4 bases of light chariots: Superior, Undrilled Light Chariots – Bow
Kushite cavalry	2 BGs	Each comprising 4 bases of cavalry: Average, Protected, Undrilled Cavalry – Light Spear, Swordsmen
Kushite archers	2 BGs	Each comprising 8 bases of archers: Average, Unprotected, Undrilled Light Foot – Bow
Kushite archers	1 BG	6 bases of archers: Average, Unprotected, Undrilled Light Foot – Bow
Camp	1	Unfortified camp
Total	9 BGs	Camp, 24 mounted bases, 22 foot bases, 3 commanders

TROOP NOTES

Three-crew Egyptian chariots are attested in the annals of Esarhaddon. Such chariots were probably pulled by 4-horses, as depicted in a drawing possibly dating from this period. We assume that the changeover from 2-horse 2-crew (light) chariots may have been gradual or incomplete.

Many of the Egyptian hereditary troops were of Meshwesh or Libu descent.

BUILDING A CUSTOMISED LIST USING OUR ARMY POINTS

Choose an army based on the maxima and minima in the list below. The following special instructions apply to this army:

- Commanders should be depicted in chariots or as cavalry.

- Egyptian close fighters can interpenetrate Egyptian archers and vice versa.
- The minimum marked * applies only if any Egyptian troops are used, the minimum marked ** only if they include any foot.

KUSHITE EGYPTIAN

Territory Types: Developed, Agricultural

C-in-C		Inspired Commander/Field Commander/Troop Commander					80/50/35	1		
Sub-commanders		Field Commander					50	0-2		
		Troop Commander					35	0-3		
Troop name		Troop Type				Capabilities		Points per base	Bases per BG	Total bases
		Type	Armour	Quality	Training	Shooting	Close Combat			
Core Troops										
Kushite chariots		Light Chariots	-	Superior	Undrilled	Bow	-	17	4-6	4-16
		Heavy Chariots	-	Superior	Undrilled	Bow	-	20	4-6	
Egyptian chariots	Only from 727	Light Chariots	-	Superior	Drilled	Bow	-	18	4-6	*4-6
		Heavy Chariots	-	Superior	Drilled	Bow	-	22	4-6	
Kushite cavalry		Cavalry	Armoured	Superior	Undrilled	-	Light Spear, Swordsmen	16	4-6	6-20
			Armoured	Average				12		
			Protected	Superior				12		
			Protected	Average				9		
Kushite archers		Light Foot	Unprotected	Average	Undrilled	Bow	-	5	6-8	6-72
		Medium Foot	Unprotected	Average	Undrilled	Bow	-	5	6-8	16-80
		Medium Foot	Protected	Average	Undrilled	Bow	-	6	6-8	0-8
Egyptian hereditary close fighters	Only from 727	Medium Foot	Protected	Poor	Drilled	-	Light Spear	4	6-8	**6-24
Optional Troops										
Kushite javelinmen		Medium Foot	Protected	Average	Undrilled	-	Light spear	5	6-8	0-12
		Light Foot	Unprotected	Average	Undrilled	Javelins	Light Spear	4	6-8	
Kushite slingers		Light Foot	Unprotected	Average	Undrilled	Sling	-	4	6-8	0-12
Egyptian cavalry	Only from 727	Cavalry	Unprotected	Average	Drilled	-	Light Spear	7	4	0-4
					Undrilled			6		
Egyptian hereditary archers	Only from 727	Medium Foot	Unprotected	Poor	Drilled	Bow	-	4	6-8	0-12
Allies										
Egyptian allies (Only before 727) – Libyan Egyptian										

75

KUSHITE EGYPTIAN ALLIES								
Allied commander		Field Commander/Troop Commander				40/25		1
Troop name	Troop Type				Capabilities		Points per base	Bases per BG	Total bases
	Type	Armour	Quality	Training	Shooting	Close Combat			
Kushite chariots	Light Chariots	-	Superior	Undrilled	Bow	-	17	4	0-4
	Heavy Chariots	-	Superior	Undrilled	Bow	-	20	4	
Kushite cavalry	Cavalry	Armoured	Superior	Undrilled	-	Light Spear, Swordsmen	16	4-6	4-6
		Armoured	Average				12		
		Protected	Superior				12		
		Protected	Average				9		
Kushite archers	Light Foot	Unprotected	Average	Undrilled	Bow	-	5	6-8	6-24
	Medium Foot	Unprotected	Average	Undrilled	Bow	-	5	6-8	
Egyptian hereditary close fighters	Only from 727	Medium Foot	Protected	Poor	Drilled	-	Light Spear	4	6-8	0-8

NEO-BABYLONIAN EMPIRE

In 626, the Chaldaean Nabopolassar (Nabû-apal-usur), governor of the Sea-Land, rose in revolt against the Assyrian Empire. By the following year he was in control of Babylon. A desultory war ensued. In 615 the Medes, under Cyaxares (Uvaxštra), invaded the Assyrian heartland. Ashur fell to them in 614. An alliance between the Medes and the Babylonians was sealed by the marriage of Cyaxares's grand-daughter to Nabopolassar's son Nebuchadrezzar (Nabû-kudurri-usur) II. The Assyrians sought Egyptian help, but this did not arrive in time to prevent the Assyrian capital, Nineveh, falling to the allies in 612. The last major Assyrian centre, Harran, fell in 610. An attempt to recover it with Egyptian help in 609 failed.

Under Nebuchadrezzar II (605–562) the Egyptians

Greek Mercenary Hoplite

were decisively defeated at the Battle of Carchemish (605), ending Egyptian attempts to regain control of Palestine and Syria. Nebuchadrezzar went on to conquer an empire including most of the territory of the former Assyrian Empire, excluding Egypt itself.

In 539 the Persians under Cyrus (Kūruš) II the Great invaded Babylonia. After winning a minor victory over the Babylonian army near Opis, the Persians were able to capture Babylon by a surprise attack by a detachment of their army while the two main armies continued to face each other off. The Babylonian King Nabonidus (Nabû-na'id) (556–539) was captured when he left his army to return to Babylon, not realising it had been taken. His army then surrendered, so that Cyrus was able to enter Babylon peacefully shortly afterwards. The Persians then incorporated all the former territories of the Babylonian Empire into their own Empire.

This list covers Babylonian armies from 626 to 539 BC.

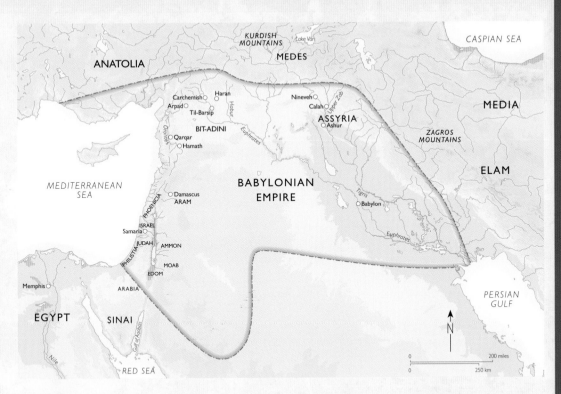

The Babylonian Empire, 6th century BC. Taken from Essential Histories 67: Ancient Israel at War 853–586 BC.

TROOP NOTES

It is clear from evidence relating to later periods that it was difficult to train troops to be equally adept with bow and spear. We therefore classify Babylonian cavalry armed with both as Bow*/Light Spear.

Some, at least, of the Babylonian foot archers were equipped with bow, spear and shield.

NEO-BABYLONIAN EMPIRE STARTER ARMY

Commander-in-Chief	1	Field Commander
Sub-commander	2	2 x Troop Commander
Chariots	2 BGs	Each comprising 4 bases of chariots: Superior, Drilled Heavy Chariots – Bow
Cavalry	1 BG	4 bases of cavalry: Average, Unprotected, Drilled Cavalry – Light Spear, Swordsmen
Skythian mercenaries	1 BG	4 bases of Skythian mercenaries: Average, Unprotected, Undrilled Light Horse – Bow, Swordsmen
Guard spearmen	1 BG	6 bases of guard spearmen: Superior, Armoured, Drilled Heavy Foot – Light Spear, Swordsmen
Greek mercenary hoplites	1 BG	4 bases of Greek mercenary hoplites: Average, Armoured, Drilled Heavy Foot – Offensive Spearmen
Archers	2 BGs	Each comprising 8 bases of archers: Average, Protected, Drilled Medium Foot – 4 Bow, Light Spear and 4 Bow
Camp	1	Unfortified camp
Total	8 BGs	Camp, 16 mounted bases, 26 foot bases, 3 commanders

BUILDING A CUSTOMISED LIST USING OUR ARMY POINTS

Choose an army based on the maxima and minima in the list below. The following special instructions apply to this army:

- Commanders should be depicted in chariots.

NEO-BABYLONIAN EMPIRE

Territory Types: Agricultural, Developed, Hilly

C-in-C	Inspired Commander/Field Commander/Troop Commander				80/50/35		1	
Sub-commanders	Field Commander				50		0-2	
	Troop Commander				35		0-3	

Troop name	Troop Type				Capabilities		Points per base	Bases per BG	Total bases
	Type	Armour	Quality	Training	Shooting	Close Combat			
Core Troops									
Chariots	Heavy Chariots	-	Superior	Drilled	Bow	-	22	4-6	4-12
Guard cavalry	Cavalry	Armoured	Superior	Drilled	Bow*	Light Spear, Swordsmen	19	4-6	0-8
Other cavalry	Cavalry	Unprotected	Average	Drilled	Bow*	Light Spear, Swordsmen	11	4-6	4-12
	Cavalry	Unprotected	Average	Drilled	-	Light Spear, Swordsmen	9	1/2 4-6	0-8
	Cavalry	Unprotected	Average	Drilled	Bow	Swordsmen	11	1/2	
	Cavalry	Unprotected	Average	Drilled	-	Light Spear, Swordsmen	9	4-6	
Guard spearmen	Heavy Foot	Armoured	Superior	Drilled	-	Light Spear, Swordsmen	12	4-6	0-6

Troop name	Type	Armour	Quality	Training	Shooting	Close Combat	Points per base	Bases per BG		Total bases	
Archers	Medium Foot	Unprotected	Average	Undrilled	Bow	-	5	6-8		0-60	
	Light Foot	Unprotected	Average	Undrilled	Bow	-	5	6-8			
	Medium Foot	Protected	Average	Drilled	Bow	-	7	6-8		0-32	16-72
	Medium Foot	Protected	Average	Drilled	Bow	Light Spear	7	1/2	6-8		
					Bow	-	7	1/2			
	Medium Foot	Unprotected	Poor	Undrilled	Bow	-	3	6-8		0-16	
	Light Foot	Unprotected	Poor	Undrilled	Bow	-	3	6-8			
Optional Troops											
Skythian mercenaries	Light Horse or Cavalry	Unprotected	Average	Undrilled	Bow	Swordsmen	10	4		0-4	
Arab levy camelry	Camelry	Unprotected	Poor	Undrilled	Bow	-	8	4-6		0-12	
Greek mercenary hoplites	Heavy Foot	Armoured	Average	Drilled	-	Offensive Spearmen	10	4		0-4	
Other levies	Mob	Unprotected	Poor	Undrilled	-	-	2	8-12		0-12	
Allies											
Median allies (Only before 550 BC)											

NEO-BABYLONIAN EMPIRE ALLIES

Allied commander	Field Commander/Troop Commander						40/25	1		
Troop name	Troop Type				Capabilities		Points per base	Bases per BG		Total bases
	Type	Armour	Quality	Training	Shooting	Close Combat				
Chariots	Heavy Chariots	-	Superior	Drilled	Bow	-	22	4		0-4
Guard cavalry	Cavalry	Armoured	Superior	Drilled	Bow*	Light Spear, Swordsmen	19	4		
Other cavalry	Cavalry	Unprotected	Average	Drilled	Bow*	Light Spear, Swordsmen	11	4		0-4
	Cavalry	Unprotected	Average	Drilled	-	Light Spear, Swordsmen	9	1/2	4	
	Cavalry	Unprotected	Average	Drilled	Bow	Swordsmen	11	1/2		
	Cavalry	Unprotected	Average	Drilled	-	Light Spear, Swordsmen	9	4		
Archers	Medium Foot	Unprotected	Average	Undrilled	Bow	-	5	6-8		0-16
	Light Foot	Unprotected	Average	Undrilled	Bow	-	5	6-8		
	Medium Foot	Protected	Average	Drilled	Bow	-	7	6-8		0-12	6-18
	Medium Foot	Protected	Average	Drilled	Bow	Light Spear	7	1/2	6-8	
					Bow	-	7	1/2		
	Medium Foot	Unprotected	Poor	Undrilled	Bow	-	3	6		0-6
	Light Foot	Unprotected	Poor	Undrilled	Bow	-	3	6		

APPENDIX 1 – USING THE LISTS

To give balanced games, armies can be selected using the points system. The more effective the troops, the more each base costs in points. The maximum points for an army will usually be set at between 600 and 800 points for a singles game for 2 to 4 hours play. We recommend 800 points for 15mm singles tournament games (650 points for 25mm) and 1000 points for 15mm doubles games.

The army lists specify which troops can be used in a particular army. No other troops can be used. The number of bases of each type in the army must conform to the specified minima and maxima. Troops that have restrictions on when they can be used cannot be used with troops with a conflicting restriction. For example, troops that can only be used "before 2500" cannot be used with troops that can only be used "from 2500". All special instructions applying to an army list must be adhered to. They also apply to allied contingents supplied by the army.

All armies must have a C-in-C and at least one other commander. No army can have more than 4 commanders in total, including C-in-C, sub-commanders and allied commanders.

All armies must have a supply camp. This is free unless fortified. A fortified camp can only be used if specified in the army list. Field fortifications and portable defences can only be used if specified in the army list.

Allied contingents can only be used if specified in the army list. Most allied contingents have their own allied contingent list, to which they must conform unless the main army's list specifies otherwise.

Egyptian Close Fighter

BATTLE GROUPS

All troops are organized into battle groups. Commanders, supply camps and field fortifications are not troops and are not assigned to battle groups. Portable defences are not troops, but are assigned to specific battle groups.

Battle groups must obey the following restrictions:

- The number of bases in a battle group must correspond to the range specified in the army list.
- Each battle group must initially comprise an even number of bases. The only exception to this rule is that battle groups whose army list specifies them as 2/3 of one type and 1/3 of another, can comprise 9 bases if this is within the battle group size range specified by the list.
- A battle group can only include troops from one line in a list, unless the list specifies a mixed formation by specifying fractions of the battle group to be of types from two lines. e.g. 2/3 spearmen, 1/3 archers.
- All troops in a battle group must be of the same quality and training. When a choice of quality or training is given in a list, this allows battle groups to differ from each other. It does not permit variety within a battle group.
- Unless specifically stated otherwise in an army list, all troops in a battle group must be of the same armour class. When a choice of armour class is given in a list, this allows battle groups to differ from each other. It does not permit variety within a battle group.

Hittite Standard Bearer

EXAMPLE LISTS

Here are sections of some actual army lists, which will help us to explain the basics and some special features. The lists specify the following items for each historical type included in the army:

- Troop Type – comprising Type, Armour, Quality and Training.
- Capabilities – comprising Shooting and Close Combat capabilities.
- Points cost per base.
- Minimum and maximum number of bases in each battle group.
- Minimum and maximum number of bases in the army.

Troop name		Troop Type				Capabilities		Points per base	Bases per BG	Total bases
		Type	Armour	Quality	Training	Shooting	Close Combat			
Chariots	Any date	Light Chariots	-	Superior	Drilled	Bow	-	18	4-6	4-24
	Only from 890	Heavy Chariots	-	Superior	Drilled	Bow	-	22	4-6	4-12
Cavalry	Only from 890	Cavalry	Protected	Average	Drilled	-	Light Spear, Swordsmen	10	1/2	4-6
		Cavalry	Protected	Average	Drilled	Bow	Swordsmen	12	1/2	0-12

(Chariots total bases: 8-24)

SPECIAL FEATURES:

- Chariots classified as Light Chariots can be used at any date. They must be organized in battle groups of 4 or 6 bases. The army must include a minimum of 4 bases of them and cannot include more than 24.
- Chariots classified as Heavy Chariots can only be used from 890 BC. They must be organized in battle groups of 4 or 6 bases. From 890 BC the army must include a minimum of 4 bases of them. It cannot include more than 12.
- The total number of bases of Chariots of both gradings in the army must be at least 8 and cannot be more than 24. Thus before 890 BC the army must have at least 8 bases of Light Chariots. From 890 BC the army can include both Light Chariots and Heavy Chariots, but they cannot be in mixed battle groups.
- Cavalry can only be used from 890 BC. They must be organized in battle groups of 4 or 6 bases. Half the bases of each battle group must have Light Spear, Swordsmen capabilities and half must have Bow, Swordsmen capabilities. The army cannot include more than 12 bases of them.

Troop name		Troop Type				Capabilities		Points per base	Bases per BG	Total bases
		Type	Armour	Quality	Training	Shooting	Close Combat			
Spearmen		Heavy Foot	Protected	Average	Drilled	-	Defensive Spearmen	7	2/3 or all	12-60
Supporting archers		Light Foot	Unprotected	Average	Drilled	Bow	-	5	1/3 or 0	6-9
Separately deployed archers		Light Foot	Unprotected	Average	Drilled or Undrilled	Bow	-	5	6-8	6-30
		Medium Foot	Unprotected	Average	Undrilled	Bow	-	5	6-8	

SPECIAL FEATURES:

- Spearmen battle groups can either be entirely of Heavy Foot Defensive Spearmen, or can have 2/3 of their bases as Heavy Foot Defensive Spearmen and 1/3 as Light Foot with Bow. If entirely of Heavy Foot they must be organized in battle groups of 6 or 8 bases. If 2/3 Heavy Foot, 1/3 Light Foot, they must be organized in battle groups of 6 or 9 bases. The total number of bases of Heavy Foot Defensive Spearmen in the army must be at least 12 and not more than 60. The total number of bases of supporting archers in mixed battle groups in the army cannot exceed 30.

- Separately deployed archers can either be Light Foot or Medium Foot. All the bases in a battle group must be of the same type, but different battle groups can be of different types. Separately deployed archers must be organized in battle groups of 6 or 8 bases. The total number of bases of separately deployed archers in the army cannot exceed 30.

- The total number of bases of supporting and separately deployed archers in the army must be at least 6 and cannot exceed 30.

Kushite cavalry	Cavalry	Armoured	Superior	Undrilled	-	Light Spear, Swordsmen	16	4-6	6-20
		Armoured	Average				12		
		Protected	Superior				12		
		Protected	Average				9		

SPECIAL FEATURES:

- Kushite cavalry can be Armoured, Superior or Armoured, Average or Protected, Superior or Protected, Average. All the bases in a battle group must have the same armour level, but different battle groups can have different armour levels. All the bases in a battle group must be of the same quality, but different battle groups can be of different quality. The list specifies the different points costs. They must be organized in battle groups of 4 or 6 bases. The army must include at least 6 bases of them and cannot include more than 20 bases of them.

APPENDIX 2 – THEMED TOURNAMENTS

A tournament based on the "Swifter Than Eagles" theme can include any of the armies listed in this book. For reasons of play balance we advise not including additional armies from other books.